For the doers.

CONTENTS

FOREWORD

Steve Balderson is one of the few filmmakers who are intelligent, well-read, *and* talented. Even more important, Steve lives by, "to thyne own self be true."[1]

This book is important for aspiring filmmakers, and perhaps those that have reached a burnout stage as well. Yes, it does contain some secrets of making the perfect film.

I've been following Steve Balderson for the last 23 years, after being introduced to him shortly after he finished his first film *Pep Squad*, which I took to Cannes and found a distributor. Several things stand out to me in looking back over these years. For me it is less about the films he has made, although they are abundant and almost always deliciously filmed. Nevertheless, that is always in the eyes and ears of the viewer.

No, the thing that stands out to me is Steve's view of life, of career, of the pursuit of goals and objectives. Those of us who make films have all faced disappointment, negative reviews and viewers who insult us. We encounter rude actors, DPs, egotistical producers and any number of other unsavory characters in the pursuit of our vision. In 23 years I've never seen Steve give up. I've never seen him lose his temper. I've watched him handle a sensitive, drama-prone actor, trying her best to "get his goat" and seen the result being that they became the best of friends.

I think the reason for this is that he has developed an ability to stay focused until the end. He remains fixated on achieving the goal and does not let small obstacles get in the way of the outcome.

I've read this book and it is very entertaining. There are some great stories. But step back from that and think about it. This is a fellow who grew up in small town Kansas, 1,500 miles from either Los Angeles or New York. We are talking about a town with a population of 3,500. He never let that hold him back. At each roadblock, he figured out a way around it. In the course of those years he became friends with countless and significant players in the motion picture business. I believe it is the fact that he has always kept his cool, never attempted to put down the other guy, and stayed firmly fixed on finishing the film, the project, the book, or whatever other goal he established for himself.

My pal and Oscar nominee, Karen Black, whom I introduced to Steve and starred in two of his movies, told me, "Steve is the most energetic and idealist director with whom I have ever worked."

That's the real lesson that Steve teaches. I'm looking forward to seeing what his path uncovers in the next decade or two.[2]

—Lloyd Kaufman
　　Founder and Chairman, Troma Entertainment Inc.

[1] A maxim created by one William Shakespeare who wrote the bestselling Renaissance book, "101 MONEY MAKING SCREENPLAY IDEAS," otherwise known as HAMLET.

[2] Since I am 75, I'll be watching from "the great movie set in the sky."

PREFACE

Steve Balderson is one of the most talented and visionary people I know. He lives, breathes and sweats creativity, as though it's built into the strands of his DNA. Aside from the nearly 20 films he's made—each one incredible and every one completely different— he's a visual artist and has hand drawn and painted his own storyboards. He's also a terrific writer, as you'll see when you read this book.

Steve's imagination knows no bounds and his intuition is off the hook. When he envisions a film project, he can already see the finished result. The first time I worked with him was in 1997; he was scoring his first film, *Pep Squad*. He'd asked Concrete Blonde's lead singer Johnette Napolitano to contribute music. He flew to Los Angeles sight unseen to meet with her. At the time, she was in the process of producing some of my work. He walked into her studio, heard a track of mine and immediately decided he wanted it for a certain scene in *Pep Squad*. My song went with the scene perfectly, describing every action. And without any editing whatsoever, to the film *or the* musical track, it fit to the millisecond.

I was blown away with the synchronicity, and after that, Steve and I both felt like soulmates. In the days before email, we'd correspond with letters that were several handwritten pages long, written and illustrated over the course of days or weeks. We went to the Cannes Film Festival together for *Pep Squad*, where he created a sensation as an up and coming American filmmaker. He also mentioned he had me in mind for a part in his film *Firecracker*, based on a true story about fratricide that had occurred in his Wamego, Kansas hometown in the 1950's. Of course, I jumped at the chance of playing Estelle, a three-breasted sideshow dancer who got sexually assaulted in a carnival trailer with the legendary Karen Black. I mean who *wouldn't*, right?

Steve also has an innate gift for choosing people that are absolutely perfect for each project, both cast and crew. Rarely does he audition actors; he has a vision of what he needs for the film. Somehow, he's able to conjure up a team that work together seamlessly for days or weeks, literally morphing into a filmmaking commune. Steve's film sets and location shoots are full of improvisation, exploration, creativity, trust, love and inevitably, lots of uproarious laughter. In my entire career I've never been on sets like Steve's, they're like a dream. There's absolutely no tension, no self-important production assistants running around all stressed out while screaming into bullhorns, no diva fits. There's just an incredibly refreshing and often transcendent feeling of teamwork. His directing is exacting, authoritative, visionary and a seamless collaboration with his actors and crew.

I could go on for hours about Steve's numerous talents, his critically acclaimed films and the way he forged ahead triumphantly in a business where it's almost impossible to succeed on one's own terms. Actually, I often think he's more like a master magician than a filmmaker, but I guess that's where the term *movie magic* comes from. And that's exactly what you'll learn in this book.

—Pleasant Gehman

INTRODUCTION

This collection of essays, stories and tales are lessons I've learned, and my experiences during the past 23 years of making and selling films worldwide.

This book is a detailed look at my style of filmmaking. As a believer that there are nearly eight billion people in the world with eight billion different perspectives, far be it for me to proclaim that this is *the* style of *all* low-budget filmmaking. I am relatively certain that other filmmakers exist in the world today and have developed their own methodologies for bringing their visual works to fruition.

My advice for you is to take whatever information I share that is useful to you and explore it. Find out if it might help you. If you come across something you feel isn't useful, don't think about it. Read on to find the next useful tip.

There are two pioneers in this world of ultra-independent filmmaking that I want to call out. First is John Cassavetes. The other is Stan Brakhage. I bring them up, not to compare myself to them, but to simply explain that from the earliest periods of film, there have always been mavericks – independent and strong-willed individuals with a story to tell, who have refused to follow the rules as they existed at the time.

John Cassavetes worked in a world of classic cinema. He was a well-respected actor who was sought after for traditional films. And yet there was another side that embraced "doing things differently." When I met Gena Rowlands (Mrs. John Cassavetes) at the Stockholm International Film Festival in 1998, where she was receiving an outstanding achievement in film award, I was struck by her comments about working in that independent environment. There was a devotion to the art and a devotion to the craft, and neither had to be compromised to reach the desired outcome.

I never had the privilege of meeting or knowing Stan Brakhage. Ironically, he was a Kansan, as am I. My mentor, Eric Sherman, was a dear friend of his. I learned about Stan through Eric and became intrigued by his work. Here was a man who explored the world of film without even subscribing to the notion that there had to be a narrative. It was an exploration of the visual sense – a journey into the brain as wired directly by the optic nerve. In addition, he was legally blind! Though I remain a committed narrative storyteller, I have been influenced greatly by Brakhage, and have explored finding my own way of using color and visuals to provoke a viewer's response.

What is the point of mentioning these two greats? It is simply this: no matter where we are, or what we have done, others have gone before us. We can derive much wisdom from their journey, and their experiences can have a positive impact upon our own journey. No, we cannot simply make their journey again. That is the ultimate problem with Hollywood – it can only emulate, copy and reproduce. Originality is lost. What we can do is be inspired and encouraged by those who have gone before.

In and of itself, the above is not enough reason to put this book together. When I embarked on my filmmaking odyssey in 1996, I was a recent CalArts dropout. I had been obsessive about filmmaking from the time I talked my grandfather out of his Betamax video camera when I was eight years old. I wanted to make films. CalArts was the right place to be if I wanted to be independent, but it was not the place to be if I wanted to dive in and experiment with narrative, live action filmmaking. Being a stubborn, 20-year-old first born, I simply quit and said to my dad, "I'm ready to make a real film." He said, "If we can do this in a businesslike manner, then yes, I will help."

What has followed, since my directorial debut *Pep Squad* was filmed in 1997, has been a series of lessons and experiences that have resulted in my approach to filmmaking. Each new project – and there have been 17 of them at the time of this writing – has taught me valuable lessons about what to do next time, and what never to do again! It is my hope that sharing all of this with you, will be of benefit to you as you move along your filmmaking journey.

STEVE BALDERSON

FINDING YOUR PERCEPTION

No two people see the same thing the same way. It's a fact. No two sets of eyes share the exact same perspective – even when we're looking at the exact same thing. Everyone on earth has an individual overall perception of everything that resides past the tip of his or her nose. Many people dislike looking past the tips of their noses – in either direction – but that doesn't change the fact that no two people see the same thing the same way. There is no such thing as a singular perspective. No overall point of view. Even when thousands of people are gathered in a convention center looking at the speaker at a podium – no two people in the room will have the same point of view. One person watches from this angle – another person watches from millimeters away. No matter how hard you try – it will be impossible to see out another person's eyes. It's just not going to happen while you're alive.

I attended film school at California Institute of the Arts (CalArts). The first thing I learned was... and my professor actually said this... "You don't need a degree to be a filmmaker – you just need to be a filmmaker." I understand that while the diploma won't be directing or producing anything, isn't it in the school's best interest to encourage me to continue attending and paying tuition?

The second thing I learned was the concept of individual perception. Upon hearing the word, the first thing I wondered was, "What is perception? Is it something to be found in a textbook? Certainly, I'll have to buy all the books and required reading. I mustn't miss a single class – just in case they pass out Perception samples. Maybe after next year's tuition payment they'll tell me what it is. Must be exciting, this Perception business, because it's certainly costly. I mean, one could purchase a Mercedes for the same price. It must be something rather extraordinary."

Well, it was. When I understood the notion of Individual Perception, it was as if an entirely new world had opened up for me. It was, in fact, better than a Mercedes. The concept is one of the most exciting, most rewarding ideas I have ever pursued. Having a core – a self – wherein *I* am in charge of what I see – changed my life.

There was a class at CalArts called Scene Analysis (or something of the sort). We watched films and took them apart shot by shot, scene by scene – inspected, from an overview floor plan (like an architectural blueprint), where the camera was positioned for each shot. We also studied where the actors were standing and where the lights were positioned.

Here's what I learned.

Hitchcock, Bergman, Tarkovsky, Buñuel, Fellini, Huston, Kubrick, and the other so-called masters, were not putting the camera in the *best* place. They weren't putting the lighting in the *best* place. They weren't telling the world's *best* stories. So, I began to wonder: "Why on earth are they so admired? What's all the fuss about? I've seen their work. I've inspected each frame down to the millisecond. What's so special about them and not other filmmakers? What do they have that others don't? Most everyone has seen a David Lynch film. Nine out of 10 people think they make no sense, have no purpose, and examine the story and don't get it, so what's the big deal?"

Well – the biggest deal is: Individual Perception. That's what they've got that no one else seems to understand. They have an Individual Perception. Special emphasis should be placed on the word INDIVIDUAL. These artists don't look at their families, friends and neighbors to answer how they ought to see something. They don't look to their schools, churches or governments for definitions on how to be or think. They simply look inward and ask themselves, "How do *I* see this?" And once they answer the question – on their own – they respond with, "If I see it like this, I shall put the camera here." They do not have other people telling them where to put the camera or how to light the scene. They answer only to their inner spirit. Their eyes tell the tale – not the eyes of the D.P., Key Grip, Focus Puller, leading actor, or Editor.

These filmmakers are masters because they are simply putting the image together as they see it. Seems easy enough. So why aren't most people doing the same thing? Why is our entire culture doing the total opposite?

I suspect that there is a reason why the notion of Individual Perception isn't taught in schools. Clearly there is a reason why the concept of having an individual viewpoint is not encouraged at church. Why? First and foremost, the concept of Individual Perception is very dangerous to those who maintain their power through prescribing what is accepted and what is not, and persuading the populace, whether it is the marketplace for movies or the voters of a nation, to a single, externally defined criteria for a group perception. Never mind that the term "group perception" is an oxymoron.

If an instructor at a university actually understood the concept of Individual Perception, it would make evaluating the work of students much more difficult. Beginning with an admission that the professor's view was not the "right and only way," it would force enormous change upon institutions of higher learning, not to mention calling their very existence into question. If society actually embraced the idea that no two people see the same thing the same way, it would revolutionize interpersonal communication. We can only imagine what would happen to movie reviews, at least as we know them. Instead of Mr. Critic proclaiming for the world what a film is about or what it means, he would actually leave it to the viewer to derive his or her own perception from the work. After all, when a viewer watches something they watch it from their own perception. They have their personal experience. Their eyes are their eyes. Mr. Critic's eyes are his eyes. Just a thought: this will likely never occur in our lifetimes. The power structure will likely see to it that the concept of Individual Perception is squashed wherever it seems to blossom. Governments, religious institutions, big business, education... you name it... have a vested interest in promulgating the notion that "one size fits all."

On my street, one size does *not* fit all. I'm about six-foot-five-inches tall and wear size 13 shoes. Average chairs don't have the right sitting distance off the floor. And even if they did, I can't sit at an average desk without ramming my knees into the low desktop. And it doesn't end there. Standard kitchen countertops are too low. The standard clothing sizes of most brands are too short, too baggy. It was like pulling teeth to get the plumber to install a shower head at the correct height for me. He said, "But this is where they put shower heads. No one puts them that high."

"I understand this, but I'd like the shower head to pour down on my face. I really don't want it to be pointing at my chest. I'm not five-foot-eight and I shouldn't have to pretend I am just so you feel better about it."

It then occurred to me that the plumber was, in fact, my height. How could he live his life never questioning this? Has he never noticed the height of his own shower head? Has he never noticed the height of his bathroom sink? Probably not. He probably has spent a lifetime defining his expectations and beliefs because THAT'S HOW IT'S ALWAYS BEEN DONE.

It amazes me that people seem to prefer just going along and letting the world define who they are and what they ought to believe. I recently got a call from a storyboard artist. He offered to sketch my storyboards for my next movie. I thought, how strange... Why would I want to shoot a film from his perspective? Wouldn't I rather use my own? My eyes are not his eyes. I mean, it's an interesting concept, to photograph someone else's vision. For me, it goes against what I define for myself as a filmmaker. If I'm not using my own perception of the material – what the hell am I doing? Lounging by the fucking pool?

Beware the people who pay lip service to the notion that there are eight billion viewpoints in the world. Even as they say that, they attempt to categorize entire nations into a single descriptive group. Muslim, Jew, Christian. All Muslims are terrorists. All Jews are rich. All Christians are good. Well, it just isn't true. In fact, growing up in Kansas we had a few Christians that... Well, there's no reason to mention their hateful Baptist church out loud.

The next time that some politician tells you to vote for him or her because they share your values, ask yourself, "how would they know what my values are?" What is so special about this politician that somehow gives them the psychic superpower to see the world through your eyes. The next time some know-it-all tells you that your script isn't traditional enough, or your short story doesn't follow the accepted structure, look deep inside and investigate/ explore with your inner self – your Individual Perception. Find out if their commentary fits your own requirements and definitions. If it doesn't, tell them to mind their own business.

Everyone would benefit by having an Individual Perception. Yet... Most people fight it. Most people do not want to have their own perceptions. They avoid developing their own unique, individualized viewpoints.

Why would anyone not want to have his or her own Individual Perception? Could it be... Is it maybe... Just maybe... People want to avoid taking responsibility for themselves? Consider this: It's so much easier to blame someone else. Somehow the world has defined responsibility as fault, and furthermore *fault* as something demeaning or negative. But the truth is – everything that happens in your life is your fault. You are responsible for your actions and reactions. YOU are responsible for YOU. Not your neighbors, churches, schools or governments.

People who don't like hearing things like that will always find an excuse to justify their behavior. Commonly, people use money as their primary excuse: "Oh, I don't have enough money to make a film..." or "Oh, I'd love to move away and be an actor but I don't have the money..." Another one is, "I'd love to work outside with my hands, but I can't afford to give up my present job." Well, then, why not figure out how to make it, be it or do it? There are ways to find investors, or a job to pay your expenses or a different and affordable lifestyle.

The second set of excuses usually deals with blaming other people. "But I can't leave my spouse and do what I want to do..." or "If I do what I want people will think I'm crazy!" Okay. Maybe so. But who is driving your car? Be aware there *are* choices.

Finally, people unwilling to take responsibility for their own behavior will use horror or abuse. "9/11 wasn't my fault! So there! You're wrong!" No, chances are, the horrific terrorist acts of 9/11 were not your fault. But ask yourself: Who forced you to stop working until 9/15? Who made you sit in front of the television? Did the terrorists? Or did you choose to do that all on your own? "I'm abused on a daily basis. It's not my fault he beats me." You are correct, it isn't your fault if you have been beaten. At least not the actual hitting. But do you make the choice to remain in that environment? Do you seek help or escape?

Everything that happens in your life is your fault. Another way of saying it is that you are responsible for determining what you do, how you do it and what your attitude toward life is. Environmental things will occur. Storms will come. Accidents will happen. Disasters will occur. But what you do, how you respond, is up to you. It's one of the first hurdles to overcome in developing your own Individual Perception. If you make the choice to not find investors, then you probably won't have any. If you make the choice to not create a business plan, you won't have one. If you make the choice to not find a job you enjoy, chances are, you will probably work at a job you hate. If you make the choice to let society define who you are, you won't be the one defining you. Is this what you want? Are these your decisions? Remember the old saying, "People who dislike having their feet sliced open should avoid walking on shards of glass."

If you want to make films, or tell a story, or work in a forest, or sit on a mountain... Well, get your shit together first. Develop YOUR point of view. Are you going to define your story by what it says in the "How to Write a Script" book? Will you define your perspective by the rules in the "Filmmaking for Dummies" manual?

According to the CIA World Factbook, men in the USA, on average, live to 72, while women live to 79. For the sake of making this less confusing, let's say the average span of a human life is 75. About 35% of it is lost in sleep. And another 30% of that is lost to the vicissitudes of youth, while 10% is probably spent being old and/or ill. That leaves about 25% of those 75 years to be all we can be, to do all we can do, and to live life as though it is as precious as it actually is. We have 18 or 19 years during which we can make choices that enrich our lives, put meaning into our relationships and advance the causes we believe in.

Just 18 or 19 years. That isn't a very long time. Every day we are given choices. Every time we look at something, whether a challenge or miracle, we are given the opportunity to either learn about it or not; to take action and do something about it or not. What will YOU choose?

On my street we praise the individual for striving. It isn't about quantitative success. After all, whose definition of success are we using? We have some simple questions on my street. "Are you happy? Are you fulfilled? Do you have a sense of reward at the end of the day? Are you meeting YOUR expectations (as opposed to those of someone else)?" And when the answers are no, which they sometimes are, we follow up by asking the following questions: "What could you do differently that would get you what you want? Is there another path to pursue that might yield different results? Are there people in the world that might help you? Have you fully defined what you want?" These questions keep me, and others on my street, focused on being responsible for our own results, not thinking wishfully about what could have been or how unfair life is. Next time you start to blame somebody else for your less than desired situation, try a couple of those questions on for size.

WHAT I LEARNED IN FILM SCHOOL

When I'm asked to speak at a film festival, or teach a class at a University, aspiring filmmakers and students always ask me what I learned in film school. Is film school worth the expense or the trouble? I always tell them it depends on their goals.

I attended CalArts from 1993 until sometime in 1996. For me, there were things I liked, instructors who inspired me, and some courses that held my attention. But there were also dreadful teachers, poorly structured courses, and experiences about CalArts that I felt were ultimately wastes of time and money.

Lots of money.

If you are considering film school and have specific questions for me, let me know. I'm happy to help. Following are the highlights of lessons I learned in film school.

LIFE LESSONS

The most significant thing I learned at CalArts was about life in general. How to function away from home, being on my own, meeting new people... and how to take responsibility for myself. All colleges are different, but when it comes to learning life lessons, I think any of them will deliver a good dose. But are these life lessons that can be learned outside of film school? Yes.

TALKING ABOUT IT VS. DOING IT

I learned more on the set of my first film than I had in all my years studying in a classroom environment. I'd been making movies since I was a child, but for the first time on a professional movie set, it all clicked and made sense in a totally different way than it had before. At film school they didn't prepare me for what it would really be like directing an actual feature. Running the set, managing actors and crew, their egos and everything else on the endless list. I learned about none of those things in film school. Of course, I didn't know that until I was out of school.

SCENE ANALYSIS

I learned how to break down a scene, draw overhead floor plans of the set, showing where the camera is, lights are, where the actors are... Was that a beneficial course? Sure. But you'll get the same thing by reading this book and listening to my talks about how to do it. And it won't cost you $40,000 a year.

MOTORCYCLES ARE OKAY

I learned that driving a motorcycle through the hallways was acceptable so long as no one got hurt. One morning about 10am, a girl named Whitney (I forgot her last name, and have no idea what she was studying) put on a Versace dress (one from his bondage collection), poured some Godiva liquor into our coffees, hopped on a motorcycle (she drove, I hung on from behind), and we rode into Tatum (the CalArts coffee shop), then roared out into the main school hallways and rode around. It was exhilarating and the engine was very loud. When we were done riding around, we went back to the coffee shop and finished the liquor.

CLOTHING OPTIONAL

I learned there was a clothing optional rule at the dorm swimming pool on campus.

SEX IS OKAY

On one of my first days at film school, on the way to my class, I noticed two people having sex in the hallway. Instructors walked by, no one stopped them. I wondered if I'd missed something in the brochure, so I asked my Dean about it. He informed me that so long as you didn't hurt anyone, you were free to do what you liked whilst at CalArts. If you don't like something you have the power to shut your eyes and turn around or walk away. That began a fascinating study into experimenting with all kinds of sexual activity. I'd slept with both men and women before CalArts, but never with an entire group. It was also common knowledge that after every art opening (which was always complete with a bar of some sort) came a kind of bizarre orgy.

CHARACTER STUDY

One of our classes had a textbook called "Men, Women & Chainsaws." We studied gender in the modern horror film. It was a great class. But, again, you can buy the book on Amazon for a lot less than a semester's tuition.

TECH STUFF

I learned that if you're interested in becoming a cinematographer (or DP), you're better off going to the Art Center in Pasadena. If you want to learn how to edit a movie, you might be better off attending a seminar on the subject for a few days. Again, an entire semester may not be worth it. Unless of course, you're interested in experiencing these kinds of life lessons.

GOING GLOBAL

I grew up in a small Kansas town, and when I returned home from film school it seemed the most logical place to begin making films. Of course, people on the coasts thought I was nuts, but where else can you close down an entire street without having to worry about the police or any passers-by bothering you?

My first three features were filmed in Kansas. It was only when I traveled to Macon, Georgia, for a film festival there, that I felt so comfortable in the town, I could see how easy it would be to make a film there. So, I did. It felt like I'd graduated to the next level somehow.

After shooting in Macon, I decided to venture even further from the roost and shoot something in Palm Springs. It was an exhilarating shoot. Partly because it's allegedly against the law to film anything inside Palm Springs city limits without having permission from the Powers That Be, permits, insurance, and all that. So, we just didn't tell anyone, and made our movie anyway.

The next year, when we were headed to the Raindance Film Festival in London, I thought, well, if we're all going to be there, we might as well make a movie at the same time. It was an absolute thrill. Much like with the California shoot, London is beyond strict when it comes to permits, insurance, and permission from the Powers That Be, and so forth. And, like our prior escapade, I decided to do it in stealth and not say a word to anyone. We got away with it.

I don't do drugs. And the rush that came with filming guerrilla style, essentially illegally, became so addictive I couldn't stop! After stealing London and Paris (for a quick scene at the Eiffel Tower), I set my sights on Hong Kong. We filmed a week in LA and then flew to Hong Kong where we filmed an additional three weeks. Hong Kong was more relaxed and filmmaker-friendly than all the other cities, but it was still under-the-radar and more than once we filmed in a location we weren't supposed to be in.

How does one accomplish these things? Well, it's pretty easy, actually. Google Earth and Google Maps makes it possible to "walk around" the streets and find locations, restaurants to eat in, alleyways to hold a staging area, and directions and times for subway travel and so forth. We didn't need to hire a location scout or send someone to take pictures. Google had already done all that for us!

It was pretty easy to post casting calls in both the UK and in Hong Kong, and all auditions were held via Skype, or on password protected YouTube or Vimeo pages.

In both cities I had great help from the actors who would appear in the film. We took advantage of shooting in areas they knew about, or perhaps places they lived. In Hong Kong, our local producer even arranged for us to film the climactic fight sequence in a penthouse with terraces and great natural lighting!

It might seem daunting at first to go to a far-flung destination and shoot a movie without ever having been there before, but I'm here to say it can be done. And, it is highly recommended. The pure joy you'll have coming home, knowing you made a movie in a foreign land... It's something you can treasure forever.

STEVE BALDERSON

THE FLOOR PLAN

Say you're building a house... would you go to the lumberyard to buy wood before drafting a floor plan? No. That would be stupid.

Now, say you want to write a screenplay. The same kind of thinking applies here, too. Screenwriters who write with no idea where they're going usually end up with a script that reads like it doesn't know where it's going.

I know several writers who sit down at their desks and stare at the blank screen (or sometimes, actual paper), dig deep for the inspiration and begin typing away. It sounds romantic. Maybe even the epitome of what it might mean to be a true writer. Well, I hate to burst the bubble, but unless you write in front of a group, no one else will see that moment except you. Sure, that romantic way of writing can sometimes make magic. But most of the time, many writers rarely make it to page three before starting over. And those who make it past page three usually take months and months to complete a single screenplay. Why? Because they didn't have a structure to follow.

Having a floor plan, or a clear outline, is a more efficient way to write a movie. There is no right way or wrong way to make this structure/outline/floor plan. A structure can be organized in any way so long as it helps you. Note cards, computer document, etc. I use a single sheet of notebook paper to begin outlining mine (in blue ball point pen). There are roughly 25 lines on a single sheet. First, number them 1-25.

Then, look at those numbers and imagine a time associated with them. I say it's somewhere between three and five minutes. Then, you can begin to separate the outline into "movie time." Your single sheet of paper now represents somewhere between 90-120 minutes. Of course, you can break it down even further, and use two sheets. I like keeping my entire outline on one sheet, making it easier to spot certain moments.

I apologize if that's bewildering. If you aren't ready to dive in and make your own outline or structure, my advice is to familiarize yourself with all the story structures you can!

One way to learn about a screenplay's structure is by drafting one for an existing movie. Any movie will do. I'd suggest watching *All About Eve* and write down a brief description of what happens every three or five minutes. Then, watch *Showgirls* and do the same. When you've finished, compare them. You'll discover they are basically the same movie. It's pretty obvious Joe Eszterhas studied the structure of *All About Eve* before writing *Showgirls*. His writing style is pretty obvious, too. But yours doesn't have to be.

Before writing my first film *Pep Squad*, I studied the structure of *9 to 5*, the classic starring Dolly Parton, Lily Tomlin and Jane Fonda. Instead of setting the story in the corporate world, I placed it in high school. And added some of my own special touches: drive-by shootings, campy dialogue, fun costumes, etc. If you study *Pep Squad* and *9 to 5*, you'll easily find the similarities in their structure.

24

If you have a structure, floor plan, or outline, you can write freely in any order you like. That's my favorite part about getting the structure down first. If there's a specific scene or sequence that's really clear to me, I'll type that out first—even if it's in the middle of the timeline. Or, maybe the ending is super clear—go write it. Details and ways to combine sequences can be decided later.

By drafting a solid floor plan, you'll have a lot of fun building your screenplay. Chances are you'll never have a feeling of burnout, you'll never have writer's block, and in the end, you'll actually have a comprehensive screenplay.

Great screenplays write themselves. Great films shoot themselves. Your job as a creator should be to never question a signal, or inspiration – just go with it. And use your eyes, ears, and then, if you've appreciated and respected your creation, it'll all be there. The skill is to not interfere with it. Give it some room to breathe.

A sentence like, "Listen to signs from the universe" might sound hokey but I would still advise it. If you've written a scene to take place inside a garage and no matter what you try, no one will let you film in their garage, simply change it. If you fight it, the fight will wear down the natural flow and keep you from seeing what is truly supposed to be there.

When you're writing a script and you hit a stumbling block, move on – go to another scene. If you've outlined your story and developed a clear structure, you can simply skip around. If you've foolishly started writing without a clear structure in place, stop whatever you're doing and develop the structure before going any further.

If you're a songwriter, and the lyrics just aren't coming to you, put in some working sounds that may or may not even be actual words. Maybe they're just noises and sounds, vowels, that you can exchange with actual words later.

Realists have a more difficult time than the rest of us because they get bogged down with the laws they were raised with. Or laws that have been pounded into them by society at large. Water is wet. The sky is blue. Neither may be actually true, but we are taught they are.

Letting go of the trappings in the world around you and allowing yourself to feel what you feel is a really hard thing to do for most people. I assure you, that once you get the hang of it, it'll be easier and easier.

In my own work, I can see the differences between projects where I've opened myself up to the universe and let all the pieces fall into place, or on the projects where I've forced it too much. It's taken me a decade to finally tap into something I can't understand, and which is hard to communicate. A beingness that is just *there*.

They say, "Write what you know." And likewise: film what you know, sing what you know, dance what you know and paint what you know. Of course, that's wonderful and always enjoyable but it's also fun to push yourself a bit into an area you don't know.

People ask me what inspires me to make a film. The answer truly lands in what I'm interested in learning next. I've never made a proper science fiction film. Or a western. Learning how to do it is exciting to me. I've never made an erotic film. Having to learn about what makes eroticism work is a challenge. Especially if it's a kind of sexuality I know nothing about.

I consider myself a mad scientist in a way. Wanting to combine different genres or starting a movie off in one tone and then ending in another. Like my film *Casserole Club*, where we began with tongues planted firmly in cheeks, then half-way through, I twisted the tone and moved into something serious, heavy and utterly devastating. I also love making movies that stick in the same tone throughout.

But regardless what story you're telling, my advice is to be open to letting the creation have its own life force. Give it some room to morph, grow, and breathe. You might just find that it grows into its own amazing being. Let it move from the cosmos *through* you into being.

Works of art are like children. And as a parent, it is most responsible to let your children develop into who *they* are. It is irresponsible for you to make them into who *you* want them to be. Take a step back and open yourself up to the possibility that they just might have their own voices and their own energies. And if you can learn to respect them, you might be surprised at what happens next.

STEVE BALDERSON

WORDS & IMAGES

Roberto Rossellini, the director, and Isabella's father, once said, "Do you know how many words it takes to adequately explain an image that will register, in your mind, the total meaning in a split second?"

I don't know the answer to his question, but my first thought is that it would take an enormous amount of words. There are endless ways to describe something. Those of us who have practiced scene analysis from already completed movies know that a simple five-minute scene might take an entire day to film. Stepping back another level, we examine the script for that scene and discover it is only a couple pages long. And when we examine the script used during the filming, we discover how little of what we see on screen had been previously written.

Films are made up of pictures, which spawn emotions and tug at our full understanding of feelings and perspective. Even when the viewer is looking at the same scene, each person will be watching it from a different history. People come from different backgrounds, different upbringings, and each have different viewpoints.

There are only a couple reasons why a screenplay should exist at all. One is to communicate to the actors what they will say and (to some degree) where they should stand, move or sit. Although the director, or each actor, may change that to suit the actual location of filming, or rhythm of the scene when it is being played out. Another purpose for a screenplay is to keep track of the skeleton of the story. If the skeleton is solid, and the foundation secure, the scenes themselves might end up in any number of possible outcomes.

It is totally possible to shoot a movie without using a traditional screenplay. If you intend to do this, my advice is to work with really great actors. Especially use actors if they have any kind of writing background or improv coaching. Actors Ethan Hawke and Julie Delpy joined their director Richard Linklater with Best Screenplay Oscar nominations for the *Before Sunset* and *Before Midnight* movies because they made those movies in this fashion.

I made *El Ganzo* in a similar way with the outstanding actress Susan Traylor and I especially enjoyed the experience working in a world like that. There is something ultimately freeing about it.

Structure is the best word I can use to describe prepping for a project like this. Each scene has a purpose. Every scene in a movie starts at A and ends at C. There will always be a B in between. Of course you can just decide whatever is the most obvious way to get from A to C and use that, but you might find there are several ways to move through B that will still lead you to C. So why not explore and also film all the alternative B's and decide in the editing room which one works the best?

You might not have the time or budget for this kind of filmmaking process, and I understand that on certain days during your shoot you might not have that kind of ultimate freedom. But my suggestion is to find that freedom whenever you can. And remember that freedom is what makes a truly independent filmmaker.

STOP WITH THE PROSE, ALREADY

Fairly frequently I'm given an unsolicited screenplay to read, to consider directing, or to give my feedback. I try my hardest to not read any of them. But every now and again, curiosity takes hold, and I'll open one up. Sometimes the scripts are filled with spelling errors, stilted dialogue, boring scenes, you name it, but there is one mistake I see most often across the board: too much ink on the page and not enough white space.

Screenplays aren't novels.

The purpose of a screenplay is entirely different than that of a novel. I could go as far as to say screenplays aren't even meant to be read. I know that might sound weird. But, think about it. What is the purpose of a screenplay? Screenplays are meant to be spoken, heard and watched.

Screenplays are a map.

They should be made up of great dialogue, with brief descriptions of specific actions that happen when nothing is being spoken.

I agree that scripts should include some prose to set the tone and hint at the atmosphere, but my advice is to keep it light. We do not need to know the year, make and model of a car, or learn about the squeaky door, or the broken windshield wipers. We just need to know it's an old, shitty car. Allow the reader to imagine whatever they want. Even then, their imagination will hinder how they interpret your story. No one will totally "get it" until they see it.

In Woody Allen's *Annie Hall*, he writes:

CUT TO:

Young Alvy at the food-stand concession watching three military men representing the Army, the Navy and the Marines arm in arm with a blond woman in a skirted bathing suit. They all turn and run toward the foreground. The girl stops before the camera to lean over and throw a kiss. The sign over the concession reads "Steve's Famous Clam Bar. Ice Cold Beer," and the roller coaster is moving in full gear in the background.

That would be much easier to read if it looked like this:

EXT. STEVE'S FAMOUS CLAM BAR – DAY

Young Alvy watches three military men arm in arm with a woman in a bathing suit.

They run towards us.

The girl stops to lean over and –

throw us a kiss.

The roller coaster is moving in the background.

By adding more white to the page, we are able to move through the description faster, getting back to the dialogue. Some might argue that Woody Allen's prose adds a different kind of atmosphere than mine does. I say that in either case, no one watching the film will ever know how it was written. And not everyone making the film is going to imagine that shot exactly as the director will see it and film it, so it doesn't matter.

When you're watching a movie you can't read what the script

says. So why not keep the paper light, effortless and easy to use?

If there is something visually specific in your screenplay that you'd like to communicate to the reader, my advice is to attach a visual design book to accompany the script. Sometimes I'll include storyboards, costume designs, even hairstyles. For my film *Firecracker*, I incorporated images into the screenplay and provided music to listen to while reading it.

Most people in the Industry will tell you never to do that. But don't listen to them. They're just stuck in a box. Do what YOU want. I did it, and it worked. Shortly after sending my *Firecracker* script to him, Dennis Hopper called me up personally and invited me to his house. When I was there Dennis told me he wanted to be in the film and added, "This is one of the best screenplays I've ever read." Perhaps his experience was enabled by the attached images and music.

I've read dreadful screenplays that made spectacular, dazzling, poetic movies, and I've read brilliant screenplays that have made terribly uninteresting movies. At the end of the day, the only thing that matters is the illustration of the vision, the poetry of the dialogue and performers who can nail it.

The first draft of a screenplay isn't the draft that gets filmed. It also isn't the version shown to the actors. It's the beginning of a long line of drafts and versions, so there's no reason why it should take you very long to do it.

I commissioned a screenwriter once for a film I wanted to make. She really struggled to complete the first draft. Weeks went by and she still wasn't finished. She said she really wanted it to be *perfect* before showing me. Yet, I knew the moment she turned it in, I would have a laundry list of notes and changes. But she kept insisting "just another week."

After I received the first draft, and started to work on my own version 2.0, she started to realize what I meant earlier. No one (but she and I) saw the first draft. And nobody needs to. It won't be published, lined with gold or shown in a museum. It's just Step One. Think of it as an instruction manual. When you're assembling a desk from IKEA, do you usually fret about Step Four until you get there? No, of course not. So, treat screenwriting the same way. One step at a time.

If you've created a good solid floor plan, writing the first draft should be effortless. When you reach a scene that doesn't seem to be working, simply skip ahead to the next. You can always go back to that tricky scene in future drafts.

Skipping ahead is the one trick to avoid writer's block. If you begin to feel stumped, move on to the next scene or sequence on your outline. If you haven't made a solid outline or floor plan yet, you should stop everything you're doing and do that first.

When I'm writing a script, my mission for Step One is: just get it off the outline and into screenwriting format (I use Final Draft software, which is industry standard). For the first draft, nothing matters yet. I sit down with my outline and just use that as my guide. Sometimes I start in the middle of the outline or jump around from scene to scene. There might be a scene in particular where the dialogue is crystal clear in my mind—I'll start there. And, sure, I've hit a wall and have had to jump past it, but I don't let it get to me. I just wait until I've expanded upon the outline.

Then, once I have taken all the information from the outline and incorporated it into my screenwriting file, even if it's patchy in places, I call that a complete first draft. Then, I "save as" and create v2.0, where I go back into the screenplay and begin to flesh out each scene more and more. When I'm confident with a nice v2.0, I'll share it with another writer or some friends for feedback. They'll either re-write some things on their own or send me notes. Then I'll "save as" and create v3.0 and repeat the process until I'm satisfied with a solid draft that will be shared with select cast, crew, another director, or producer.

And, naturally, each of them will want to chime in with their "two cents." Sometimes their notes are silly, but sometimes they could have a brilliant idea that can help you. When that happens, take it. This isn't about you; it's about the greater good for the project. And if that note or change fits in with your model of the world you're creating, why not use it? No one will ever know where it originated.

I was given advice about feedback and notes from the rock star Jane Wiedlin from the Go-Go's, a very successful singer, songwriter and music producer. She told me her process for reacting to notes and feedback. First, look at the note. Ask yourself if it fits within your model of the world you're creating. If the answer is No, ignore it and simply move on to the next note. Ask the question again. If this time the answer is Yes, then ask yourself a subsequent question: "If I implement this note, will it make me look like a genius?" If the answer is No, then perhaps move on, but if the answer is Yes – you might consider making the change. Again, no one will ever know where it originated.

Once you find yourself working on version 12, you'll kick yourself for wasting so much time on v1. Remember this lesson next time you complete your outline and are ready to begin writing the scenes and dialogue. If you can get into a rhythm where you don't think too much about writing, and you just write, you'll find that it's possible to complete the first draft of a screenplay in no time at all.

Remember: no one sees the first draft. There is no reason to give yourself any kind of pressure when you're conceiving it. Give that formation time to grow and what might seem messy at the beginning will begin to make sense. Each story takes on its own life force and if you are open to the inspiration around you, and live with a "create now, edit later" mindset, your screenplay will be complete in no time.

When you're writing a screenplay, it's a good idea to name each character who has a line of dialogue. Even if the character in question is only the "Workman" or the "Church Lady." I think every role deserves a personality even if their characters names aren't ever spoken. It's a good habit to build. Why?

Actors like to have names. It's much more fun to be in a movie when you're playing "Cheryl" instead of "Woman #3." Furthermore, it looks better on the actor's resume if they played a person who is named, instead of playing a mere number. Think about it from the standpoint of a director or producer. When you're casting an actor to play the "Bartender," do you pay more attention to actors who have played "Man 2" or those who have a part called "Carl" on their resume?

Which following resume suggests the person is a better actor?

FILM	ROLE
Night of the Bees	Jackie
Hungry for Love	Rose
Tomorrow, My Sweet	Kathy

Versus:

FILM	**ROLE**
Night of the Bees	Woman in Alley
Hungry for Love	Flower Shop Employee #2
Tomorrow, My Sweet	Travel Agent

Unless the actor is playing "Man 2" in the latest Spiderman movie, chances are the movie titles on people's resumes won't mean much. For a big budget studio action movie, they probably see thousands of men for "Man 2," so if this guy got picked, he must be great! Whereas, say the actor played "Man 2" in a no-budget indie that you've never heard of... what message does that send? Did they use him because they couldn't get anyone else, or is he a decent actor? Now, if he'd played "Roger" in that same indie movie, I'd be more apt to consider him.

When I'm casting a new movie, budget or no-budget, I always make sure to go through the script and give every character a name whenever possible. I understand when there's a scene, say, involving a drug bust, it would become problematic to name every single policeman in the scene. So in that case, it's okay to refer to the group as "Policemen." But, if there are a couple cops that have a line or two, why not give them names? "Officer Thad," or "Officer Dave" looks a lot better during your end credits, and also on their resumes, than "Officer 1" and "Officer 2."

Can't think of a name? No need. Sometimes, I'm fresh out of names in my imagination database, too. When that happens, I grab an old 1990's New York City telephone book stolen years ago from a hotel before they went out of print. I look up at the ceiling, flip through the pages and stick my finger in. I'll rest it firmly on a page, then open the page to find out what name I pointed to. Usually, I'll use whatever name I've picked. I'll try it now.

Let's say I need a name for a waitress. Okay, I'm opening the NYC telephone book, and... *point.*

Ronda. What a great waitress name. I think I'll just use that.

I also need a name for the short order cook in the back. Okay, I'll open the phone book, and... *point.*

Thomas. Okay, that's fine. I could use "Thomas," but I was hoping for a name with a little more feeling. I'll try again... and... *point.*

Delbert. Totally sounds like the cook in the back of the diner.

See, not hard at all. It helps when you use a phone book from a big city so there will be many cultural names. Finding a big telephone book might be impossible now, so anytime you come across a phone book, drop it into your suitcase before checking out.

HOW TO READ A SCREENPLAY

I never read other people's screenplays unless I understand *how* to read them. By what perspective to read them. It's a waste of time otherwise. A lot of people read screenplays left and right, but have they ever stopped to think about from what perspective they are reading it? When was the last time you read a screenplay you didn't write? How did you read it? No, not "at bedtime," or "with the lights on," I mean... from what perspective did you read it? Were you looking at it through the gaze of a producer, or a writer, or an actor, or a director, or a composer?

Recently, a filmmaker sent me the first 10 pages of a script and asked, "Can you tell me if you think this has potential?" I thought, well, it's impossible to measure the value of a screenplay in the first ten pages. I might be able to get a sense of the writer's style, their use of vocabulary, whether their dialogue is lyrical or stilted, or even an example of the tone and atmosphere of the story, but feature screenplays are usually around 90-100 pages. Judging a screenplay in the first 10 pages is a bit like licking the outside of an apple to determine the taste without biting into it. And people who have tried both Granny Smith and Gala apples can tell you that neither tastes like a Fuji. So, licking it just won't cut it.

I answered the filmmaker: "Before I read it, tell me what is the perspective I'm reading it from... A director's perspective? A writer's point of view? Or, a consultant's?" The filmmaker replied, "Great question. Read it first as a director."

To clarify further, I asked another question: "As if I were directing (which would mean I would only see if the story was something that spoke to me personally as an artist, and judge the story based on that alone)? Or, do you want me to read it from the perspective of you directing (which means that I would not read it from my perspective, but rather, project an outward, external view and imagine this filmmaker's personality—how he sees the world—and does this story seem to align with his sensibilities)? Or, am I supposed to read it from the standpoint of Ron Howard directing (which means I'd be thinking about it from a totally different place—would Ron Howard's sensibilities help this story appeal to a broad audience, and would studios find this story appealing financially)?"

The filmmaker answered in a tongue in cheek manner, which ended the discussion, but I was totally serious. I decided to not read the 10 pages he sent to me. Even if he had sent me the completed screenplay, I wouldn't have read it without understanding from which perspective to read it. If everyone practiced this way of thinking and consciously reading, it would change the industry.

It's impossible to adequately judge a movie's potential by the screenplay alone. Screenplays aren't novels, and what's on paper doesn't always translate visually. Film is the director's medium. To judge a movie one must always take into consideration the visual elements: costumes, hair styles, make-up, art direction, production design, props, camera work, colors, rhythm, performers and their acting abilities and especially music and score.

Take this for an example: *The Wizard of OZ* was gloriously colored and staged, while 1985's *Return to OZ* was dreadful looking (never mind the bleak storyline, I'm talking the lack of good design and sleek direction). I imagine the people reading *Return to OZ* had in their minds the kind of thing that made the first film so cherished, but were devastated upon viewing the end result. There are also brilliantly visualized shows like Broadway's *Wicked*, and the latest film installment, *OZ: The Great and Powerful*, which looked incredible. It's all about aesthetic understanding and good taste.

Part of the director's job is to translate the written word into visual storytelling. A great assignment for a class in film school: Everyone gets the same script, and we'll see what happens when they turn in their projects. One director will take the same story and deliver something totally opposite what another director will do. Yet both films will originate in the same words.

Instead of reading screenplays, I ask for either a complete plot or synopsis (not one meant to lure me into buying the movie, but rather the entire detailed story in just a couple of pages, including spoilers and climax, ending, etc.). Usually if the structure is there, and the story is solid, it is possible to make the screenplay great (even if, at that stage, it isn't fleshed out). But if the structure is not solid, the movie won't work. No matter how scenes are re-written, or how dialogue is changed here and there, until that structure is defined and made solid, it just won't work.

Eight times out of ten, this is the case with most screenplays. This is why I ask for writers to share with me the structure first. Why should anybody have to waste time reading an entire screenplay only to discover three hours later that there is no structure? It's a lot easier and less time consuming to just read a few paragraphs first. Then, if there is a solid structure, dive into the screenplay and enjoy it. But remember to ask yourselves: from which perspective am I reading this? Am I going to read this as a viewer? A filmmaker? A distribution executive? A marketing executive? An actor? Or simply for entertainment?

EVERY FILM IS REALLY THREE

Did you know that every movie is actually made up of three different movies? By the time you've seen it, the film you're watching has gone through metamorphosis at least three times. I'm not talking about different endings, re-shoots, and the like. I'm talking about how the film changes its form between conception to screening.

At first there is the film you write, then it evolves into the film you shoot, and next it evolves yet again in the film you edit. At each of those moments there exists a different film. Sometimes the differences between each step can be extreme. Sometimes, the transitions are more subtle. But it is a fact that no movie remains the same as it first appeared on paper by the time you reach completion of the image.

First-time filmmakers usually struggle with this. Panicking about how to capture every line exactly as it's written (and if they wrote the script, that emotional tie is even stronger). Yelling at actors until they get it perfect. Making them do 20 takes because they keep forgetting *that one word*. Fighting with an editor because he shifted some lines, rearranged some scenes, or got rid of them entirely.

I know I struggled with this when I started, but no one bothered to tell me this until after I'd made a few movies. Suddenly, one day, I heard, "There is the film you write, the film you shoot, and the film you edit." It was an Ah-ha moment. It was like a new world of possibility and freedom opened up. Learning how to adapt into this way of thinking has helped me strengthen each step of the process. My screenplays have benefited, my on-the-set shooting time is more productive, and the post-production and editing process comes together seamlessly.

There will always be a word in a screenplay that an actor changes, forgets, or the editor removes. There will always be a sequence that flows differently when acted out than when it was imagined on paper.

Opening yourself up to the metamorphosis in the process will present opportunity when you least expect it.

On a recent film project, I had a scene that included the prop of an actress blowing bubbles. You know, the toy kids use made up of soapy water that, when you stick the wand in and blow through, creates bubbles that float around the room. Well, I found the perfect bubbles set on eBay for $2.95. So, I ordered them.

When they arrived, I was shocked to find a plastic gun that shoots bubbles and glows with plastic LED lights. Instead of sending it back, I thought, well, this was supposed to happen. I was meant to use this in the movie. And, you know what, the scene worked out so much better with the bubble gun then I'd have ever imagined.

Had I been the kind of hard-nosed writer/director who wanted to stick to the written word, I'd have sent the gun back and demanded the bubbles I'd originally ordered. And, had I done that, sure, the scene would've played out as it was written on paper, but, it would not have been as exciting as how it ended up with the bubble gun.

The other thing I like to do when shooting is keep the writer from ever visiting the set. For me personally, I like the freedom to focus my perception on the translation of the material without having someone's eyes over my shoulder the entire time.

Frankie Krainz is a brilliant screenwriter I've worked with multiple times. And I respect him as a person on top of that. He always insisted he'd keep to himself, quietly in the corner, but could he please visit the set. I explained to him that even if he did keep quiet, I would be aware of his presence, and that a voice in my left ear would constantly be second-guessing everything I was doing. What would Frankie think about that? How is Frankie feeling about this? To prevent that distraction and any loss of my own confidence, I decided to make it a rule to never have the writer of the project appear on set while filming.

My advice is to keep oneself open to any possibilities of change along the way. From writing, to filming something differently than it was written, to editing a scene in a totally new way. Once, I re-wrote a scene in the editing room to spectacular results. Putting the first line third, and the second line first, and so on. It is fascinating what can happen if you're open to the possibilities.

FILMMAKING INTENTION

Another thing I learned in film school happened one day out of the blue. It suddenly occurred to me how to communicate and see something from outside myself. As an observer.

I was in a class—yes, I know, shocking—I'm not sure which class, but the assignment was to create something horrific. Many students created images filled with frightening subject matters, blood, fear, horror, all the aspects of something most people would agree to usually define as horrific for the viewer. Well, one student returned with an image of a vase of daisies. Especially nice-looking tall-stemmed crisp white daisies, bathed in sunlight on a perfectly nice day.

The teacher chastised the student for failing the assignment, but I kept wondering if this vase of pretty daisies wasn't somehow—for the artist—the most accurate illustration of something horrific. In defense of the artwork, the student confessed to the teacher (in front of the entire class) of having been brutally raped as a teenager. And during the attack, the only item in their field of vision was this pretty vase of daisies.

The teacher consoled the student and commended the courage it must have taken to conquer those deepest, most horrific moments, in order to create the artwork, but said that it was still a failure. A failure? Naturally, the rest of us spoke up in defense of the abused student.

The teacher simply said, "Think about it from the point of view of the viewer. What does the viewer see? It doesn't matter what the maker is thinking if he or she doesn't communicate that to the audience." The teacher was right. None of us knew how horrific the daisies were until we knew the whole story.

There are a variety of ways the artist in question could have communicated this in a clear way. Even while keeping the sunshine and pretty daisies, maybe add a crack in the vase, with a little blood dripping out. Or, paint the attack in the background, hidden in the shadows, so that we don't immediately see the attack at first glance. There are numerous ways to show it horrifically and still maintain the original concept.

In this case, the artwork was a disappointment. Although the student's intent was there, the student failed to communicate it. It really taught me how to see something from another person's point of view. When I create a film, I'm thinking about how a scene feels from a variety of angles. Or, how certain people will respond to certain things. Learning how to do this has helped me a great deal. Here's the lesson:

The meaning of communication is what the other person feels, sees, or hears—not solely on what you say, do, or show.

It is true in art, in film, and it's true in life. Understanding that sentence will be like discovering a top-secret document or a hidden treasure. Just try it out and see what I mean.

I worked with a PR person once who was a horrible

communicator. His focus was inward; his objectives were to hear himself speak, to say what *he* needed to say. From his point of view, his communications were a success. And when someone wouldn't respond to him, it was always that other person's fault. Never his.

I often told him the meaning of communication is what the other person hears—not what you say; and I asked him how he could change his communication in order to get what he wanted. He'd look at me like I was speaking a language from outer space. In the end, I decided to work with someone else. Sometimes people are so far in their own head it's impossible to help them get out. I hope this isn't the case with you.

Every person is different. Actors, designers, clients, friends, neighbors... Each person takes in different words in different ways. If you can learn how to go outside of yourself, imagine the other person's perspective of what you're saying, or what you're showing them, it will change the way you communicate. It dissolves stress, misunderstandings, and evaporates conflict. And it'll make you, and those around you, a lot happier.

STEVE BALDERSON

NEED STARS?

A question a lot of aspiring filmmakers face is whether or not to cast movie stars. Do movie stars help your film get funding? Do stars mean you'll get a solid distribution deal? Does it mean your film will be successful? I'm here today to tell you that it's all a myth, and it doesn't matter a bit. Nope. Not at all.

Certain people in the Industry will tell you that it is totally necessary to have a movie star in your movie. If a distributor tells you, chances are their motivation truly stems from laziness. If there's a star in your movie, they don't have to work hard to sell your movie. In fact, it won't matter what your movie is about, because they'll just pitch it to buyers as a "so-and-so" picture.

If it's an Industry executive looking to produce your movie, they'll say it's important because it looks good on their resume if they worked with "so-and-so" instead of someone they've never heard of. Aspiring actors will do the same. Some actors will even showcase that famous person in their reels in hopes to appear more qualified than they actually are. Tricking directors into thinking "Wow, she starred with Julia Roberts, she *must* be important."

Truth is, it doesn't matter whether there are stars in your film or not.

My first film *Pep Squad* has no stars in it. Yet, it was critically acclaimed and licensed for distribution in nearly every country on Earth.

When searching for investors on my second film, one of the actors cast was Dennis Hopper. Surprisingly, even with Dennis Hopper attached, we couldn't find funding in order to make it. I ended up replacing him with the musician Mike Patton (Faith No More, Mr. Bungle), and suddenly we had funding.

My film *Watch Out* starred a few recognizable faces that were previously in other recognizable projects (Peter Stickles from *Shortbus*, for example), but none of them were "stars" per se, and when that film came out, it debuted at number 27 on Amazon's Top 100.

And then there's my film *Stuck!* which starred Mink Stole, Karen Black, Pleasant Gehman, Susan Traylor and Jane Wiedlin in a women-in-prison movie—all together! I mean, one would think that would be an easy sell, right? Well, it didn't sell as well as *Pep Squad* or *Watch Out*. It was a black and white noir film paying homage to a 1950s style of filmmaking. Perhaps some buyers didn't get it on a commercial level.

So, you see, it does not matter who is in your movie. What matters is that your movie is well made with a captivating story and solid performers. We have all loved a movie or two starring a cast of no one we recognize.

Remember that when casting your next film. Stars do not always bring in money. But they can sometimes cost a lot of it.

If you decide you do want stars, you'll have to deal with their agent or manager. The experience communicating, if you can call it that, with an agent or manager is, beyond a doubt, one of the most illogical and total wastes of time I've ever known.

Don't be afraid of calling a famous actor's agent or manager. It is true that most of them are nasty people who do nothing to help their clients, and in some cases make their clients look bad. But if you know they're going to be rude before you call them, it'll make your experience at least entertaining. And then calls with professional, polite people will come as a relief.

I'd avoid calling the likes of Anjelina Jolie or Tom Cruise. My advice is to pick actors who are kinda famous but aren't the super elite movie stars. Say, Mary McDonnell.

Earlier, I asked someone if the actress Mary McDonnell sounded familiar. "Remember the woman who was in *Dances with Wolves*?" Nothing. "She was nominated for an Oscar." Nope, not a clue. "She was also in Independence Day." Nope, nothing.

So, we're talking about actors that have strong talent, but that aren't selling movie tickets based on their name alone.

Recently, an associate of mine made a list of some actors to approach for a project. Some of them are better-known, and others are strong actors who are well-known in certain groups but whose names are totally unknown by most of the movie-watching public.

My friend shared with me his experiences talking to agents. One agent hung up on him in the middle of explaining there would be deferred payment. Now, I understand that some actors have gambling addictions, alimony payments, and whatnot, and they simply cannot afford to work for deferred pay. I understand that. But, what I don't understand is the impulse that makes it okay for an agent to hang up in the middle of a sentence. That's just rude, and totally unprofessional. Somehow it would kill them to say "No, thank you."

Another thing that is curious about calls to agents—it doesn't matter how famous their clients are. In some cases, the lesser known the actor, the ruder the agent. Which sparks questions.

Is that why we haven't seen that actor in so long? Is the agent being rude to everyone who calls? My hunch is that most actors have no idea how awful their agents treat people. They should know because it makes them look bad, too.

I was reminded of an earlier experience I had calling agents.

Once I contacted a representative for Deborah Harry ("Blondie"). Her representative told me off in a very condescending manner. I shared the story with the actor James Russo, who laughed and promptly gave me Debbie's home phone number. I called her up, told her what had happened, and she was furious. She made that representative call me to apologize for his behavior.

Did she know he was doing that? I don't know. She knows now. I wonder how many actors and performers out there are missing great opportunities because their agents and managers are unprofessional. Probably quite a lot.

There are thousands of famous actors who are not working very often. I cannot imagine that all of them are waking up in random bedrooms claiming aliens have abducted them. No, my hunch is that part of the reason they are off the radar is that they are being represented by people who don't understand how to communicate like grown-ups.

If you are seeking representation, either as a director or actor, please have a discussion to define their job. Do you want to build a barricade? Is your agent or manager a means to *prevent* people from communicating with you? If so, that is fine, just define it. If you want your representative to act as a mediator or negotiator, my advice is to pick somebody who will behave as such.

If you are seeking celebrities for your project, my advice is to avoid agents altogether and find a way to reach the actor directly. Creative people are more interested in the creation. Agents and managers are only really interested in their commission.

Lately, there has become a huge controversy about actors buying roles, thanks to certain perks on Kickstarter and Indiegogo. I understand the perspective of people who are against this sort of thing, but I can also understand the perspective of people who don't think it's a big deal. Like me.

As an independent filmmaker, I need funding in order to make a movie. The amount of funding is irrelevant. Even if you plan to shoot a movie for no money, or you aren't paying anyone, you'll still have to buy hard drives to store footage, and put gasoline in your car to move from one location to the next. If someone comes along and says, "Hey, I can give you some money, but will you put me in the movie," my response is, "Of course!" If I said, "No, I'm morally against that sort of thing," chances are I won't be able to make my movie. Or it'll take longer to find the funding needed, and I'll be wasting time.

I make sense of it by thinking about it as an investment. Even if the person giving (i.e. donating) money on a crowd funding website isn't "investing" per se, they are investing in their careers. How it is any different to spend $2,000 on headshots and acting classes when you can skip all that and just buy a role with it?

And in that same thinking, what's the difference between that kind of process and someone like Jodie Foster producing a script for herself to star in? I can't think of one.

I know that if Stanley Kubrick was still alive and running an Indiegogo campaign for his new film, and for a significant donation, I could go and be his script supervisor for two months, without being paid, fed, or housed, I'd jump at the chance. And if I couldn't afford it, I'd encourage any other filmmaker who could, to do it. One would learn more in that experience than attending all the best film schools combined, and it would probably cost a lot less.

If that scenario were true, some might say it's unfair because all the script supervisors are out of work because I bought the job away from them. I do not feel badly about it. After all, only one of them would have been hired to begin with. A production doesn't need to hire *all* of them. So, I say, what difference does it make?

Likewise, when an actor buys a role, all the other actors out there who could've auditioned are now out an opportunity for work because somebody else bought their part.

A famous actress once said, "Success isn't something you're given, it's something you take."

Going back to the Jodie Foster scenario. Was she waiting around for someone else to develop and produce, and then cast herself as, *Nell*? Nope. She took the initiative and did it herself. There are people out there who blame her because she has "privilege" because she's a superstar, and all that. How is her kind of privilege any different than someone who could afford to buy a job as script supervisor, or an actor who can afford to buy a role? None so far as I can see. Yet, why is it okay for celebrities to develop and cast themselves in parts, and it's not okay for an unknown person to buy one as a perk?

Is the backlash pointed towards the moral integrity of the person making these crowd funded movies? Take me, for instance. If I did a Kickstarter campaign, and offered a perk that for $X you could be my script supervisor, would you call me a villain? Would you say I'm out to take advantage of people? I understand I'm not Kubrick, which is why my perk would cost a donation considerably less than his. But I can assure you that the person who bought that perk would learn more on my set than spending $X on seminars, books, classes, or anything else. Therefore, it's a fair trade. They're helping me, and I'm helping them. It's a mutual arrangement, and one that I think is just fine.

STEVE BALDERSON

MUSICIANS ARE FAMOUS, TOO!

The film business is one of the most illogical businesses in the world. Or, rather, the people who operate inside The Industry (executives, let's say) make some of the most illogical decisions on a daily basis. I imagine if they were working in any other field of business, they would likely be fired and out of a job pretty quick.

And, well, actually, the turnover rate for Industry executives is steadily climbing. Remember your contact at that company? Yah, he only worked there for six months and then he was canned. Now he works at that other company. No, wait, that company folded, I heard he's working as a Producer's Rep now.

Anyway, when I'm casting a movie, I've found that sometimes it makes more sense to cast famous musicians in roles instead of famous actors.

Famous musicians have global followings and fans who buy whatever they churn out. I figure tapping into that marketplace makes sense if my purpose is to have exposure *and* sales. To get the movies I make out there and be seen by an audience. I do not make movies so they can sit on the shelves in a dark closet.

Did you know that a musician can have as many, and in some cases, even *more* fans than a famous actor? Famous actors are familiar with being in movies. When I'm putting together a guerrilla style shoot, the chances of attracting someone like George Clooney to that project is pretty slim. On the other hand, famous musicians aren't approached to be in movies very often, so for them it's a fun adventure.

Danny DeVito can attest that Mike Patton has as many fans as he does. Ask him! However, most Industry executives do not know who Mike Patton is. And, those who do know probably don't think he has a fan base as big or larger than Danny DeVito. So, when you have a film starring Mike Patton, Industry executives will not be as interested as they would if your project starred Danny DeVito.

I learned that lesson when peddling my film *Firecracker*. I was just stunned by the film Industry's total disregard for famous musicians. I was reminded by this again while peddling my film *The Casserole Club*, which stars "Backstreet Boy" Kevin Richardson in his film acting debut.

"The Backstreet Boys" are *the* best-selling boy band of all time. They've sold over 100 million albums. They have a global following that is larger than that of Mike Patton. Which means, Kevin Richardson has more fans than Danny DeVito and Mike Patton combined. That kind of following is the equivalent of having someone like George Clooney in the movie. The tens of millions of "Backstreet Boy" fans spend money to buy a movie just as easily as they do music.

Yet most film businesses cannot wrap their heads around this idea.

But that's okay. You don't particularly need anyone in the film business to help you market directly to a musician's fan base. You can do it on your own.

Filmmakers: think about why you're making a movie. Do you want people to see it? Are you only interested in working with famous actors? Have you thought about casting a famous musician? Did you know that there are famous musicians you've never heard of who have more fans than Brad Pitt?

Maybe one day the film Industry will recognize the music industry exists and take advantage of cross-market promotion. But until they figure it out, my advice is to take advantage of it, and be thankful they aren't so you can reap the rewards!

Going back to my earlier point about the HollyApple Turnovers. I don't mean traditional apple turnovers, which are tender and flaky, with apple pie-like filling and a thin, white glaze. Nor am I speaking about Gwenyth's daughter. I'm speaking of the kinds that are just a bit flaky and work as executives at movie studios and production companies in Hollywood.

When I began my film career in the 1990s, I met a slew of awesome people who had great jobs with all the major studios. After now-disgraced producer Harvey Weinstein called me personally to express his interest in acquiring my film *Pep Squad*, I became friends with his assistant. Or, rather, his assistant du jour. That person was quickly replaced by another assistant, who, shortly after being hired, developed a crush on me. It was kind of bizarre. Of course I never met the guy in real life, but to be funny, I sent him an 8×10 glossy headshot of my face as a joke. He hung it up on the wall by his desk. And each time I called to visit with Harvey, the assistant thought I was calling to visit with *him*, not Harvey. It all became very confusing. But, just as soon as he was developing some long-distance feelings for me, he was axed as well. So, in came another assistant. By that point I'd sold my movie to another distributor, so I stopped calling. I'm not sure who his next assistant was. Probably someone who enabled Harvey's now known infamous and repulsive behavior.

My mentor Eric Sherman always suggested it was a really good idea to network and make friends with executives at certain companies because at some point, they might be able to help me get a movie made, or whatever.

Besides the aforementioned assistant, I met some great people who were VPs of production, directors of acquisitions, and other higher-ups that, one would think, would be relatively great connections.

One incredible woman, Sara Rose, was an inspiration to me. After seeing my film at the Cannes Film Market, she came up to me afterwards to introduce herself. She told me to stop by and see her at MGM any time I was in LA. And I did. She always took my meetings and was always a delight to visit with. She then became Senior VP of Production at MGM/UA and we spoke many times about making my film *Firecracker* together. That didn't happen, but we kept in touch and I always looked forward to working with her in the future.

While I was on track to develop these relationships (some of the people were awesome, like Sara Rose, but some of the other ones were the flaky kind and not so cool), a strange thing kept happening. They kept losing their jobs.

Some executives moved to other companies on their own free will, some were moved into different jobs within the same company (but not a job that had anything to do with why I was talking to them), and then there were some who were fired and never seen or heard from again.

After several years it became clear to me that most movie executives can't keep a job for more than about two years. This Turnover Syndrome is a bizarre fact about the movie business. Even Penny Marshall mentioned this phenomenon in her memoirs. If there is someone working with you on your movie when you start the process, they won't be working at the studio when you finish the movie. Just as simple as that.

My question is: why? Why can't most movie executives keep a job for more than a couple years?

STEVE BALDERSON

TOP OR BOTTOM?

There are two ways to budget your movie. The first, which is known as the traditional way all movies are budgeted, is Bottom Up budgeting. Bottom Up budgeting is the most ineffective way to budget a movie, yet most everyone does it.

Bottom Up budgeting is where you start from ground zero with no idea what your movie is going to cost. Then you identify all the people, jobs, things you think you need, and at the end you'll have the amount that the movie will cost. There is software out there, which can help you approach it this way.

When using this software, you'll scroll an endless list of job titles, learning about jobs you never even knew existed, but now that you know about them, you *must* have on your crew. That is your first mistake. A Script Supervisor would be great. $1,000 per day is a bit much so you plop in $500 per day. Then you'll go to the next job, plop in a new amount, and so on. At the end, the software will tally up all the jobs and expenses, and voila: you discover the budget for your movie is $2,450,000.

Now you're faced with the unlikelihood of raising that kind of money. Which, if you can do it, great, by all means, have at it! Chances are it simply isn't going to happen. You might raise a fifth of that, or even less... but two million?

I prefer to budget a movie using a Top Down approach. This is where you start with an amount you think you can raise and deduct items you know you can afford, and do away with the items you can't or don't need.

Say we believe we can raise $175,000 to produce the movie. Or, let's say we have already raised $130,000 and we're not sure that's enough. I'm here to tell you $130,000 is more than enough, and here's how you'll do it.

First, identify the items you *must* have. Not things you *think* you need. You don't need a Script Supervisor. Anybody on your crew can do it – since the job is required only when cameras are rolling. If you're making a film that requires visual effects or special effects make-up, those items are mandatory. So, write those down and subtract their cost (let's say $12,500). Now you only have $117,500 remaining in your budget.

Next up, fifteen people on the cast and crew. Let's say you'll shoot for two six-day weeks and pay everyone $200 per day. Subtract $36,000. Now you only have $81,500 remaining. Can you get some of those people to work for deferred pay or "points"? If so, you can add $10,500 back into your budget. Need to fly them anywhere? Subtract those costs, or find out if you can find someone who might donate their airline miles in exchange for a free ticket and add those costs back in.

Hopefully you understand where I'm going with this. I'm thinking about expenses as if I were using a debit card. Not a credit card. I understand the general public would rather use a credit card instead of a debit card. The traps of "buy now, figure out how to pay for it later" are easy to fall into. But those people are usually in debt.

By handling your budget in the Top Down approach; you'll know exactly how much money you have and can make realistic decisions on what you can afford. And what you can't. Which will keep your movie on budget, and you won't waste a cent.

CUT OUT THE FAT

If you have a backer with unlimited financial resources like, say, a pharmaceutical company, then this doesn't apply to you (i.e. Studios). But for the rest of the filmmaking world, think about this. People cost time and money. Even people working for free.

Every single person on your crew will cost a certain amount of money. That amount varies, of course, because maybe you're housing people at friends and neighbors. But if you aren't, you're going to have to house them someplace. Cheap motels aren't free. Some people have the ability to fly or drive to you, feed themselves, and bring their own bottled water to the set. But will everybody? Probably not.

The easiest way to save time and money is to cut out unnecessary crew positions. If you operate your own camera, you don't need a camera person. If you know about lighting, you won't need a DP. You don't need a Gaffer, because anybody can hold the reflector or turn on the light. Go for an intern. If you have a DP or camera person, it usually means you'll add another dozen or so people automatically. Most DPs and camera people can't manage to hold the camera and also pull focus, change lenses, memory cards, download cards, etc., and they will usually request an additional person for each of those simple activities. And all of those people will have nothing to do but stand there and wait for their specific duty.

By having the actors manage their own costumes and props, you omit the need for a props person, props assistant, costumer, seamstress, and whomever else those people *need* to assist them in order to do their jobs. Of course, if you use a costume person, consider another area on the crew you can omit a person. Can that costume person also manage being on Script during the takes (since they'd otherwise be doing nothing)?

By keeping on schedule and adequately planning ahead of time, you'll also omit the need for a Second AD, and any other office-type person who would otherwise have nothing to do but sit around all day waiting to see if you're behind schedule.

In addition to saving money, by omitting unneeded crew people, you'll also save time. The more people you have, the more time it takes for everyone to show up. More people means less time in the loo (so "take 15 minutes" usually turns into "it's been 45 minutes, we're already behind, and not everyone has had a chance to use the toilet.")

When an aspiring film student comes up to me and says, "I want to work on your crew, I'll do anything, I'll even pay my own way," it's very tempting to have them join the team. But I've learned to draw the line. While it's helpful if one or two people come aboard under those circumstances, six or seven end up bogging down the set.

In addition to saving time and money, a smaller set is more enjoyable. If you've never been on a film set before, you'll come to love the days when hardly anyone is there. Fat or thin, tall or short, the fact is, people take up space.

Add in equipment cases, bags, tripods, even at the barest minimum, it becomes crowded really quick. And, a crowded hallway isn't as easy to walk down as an empty one. Getting on and off the set, or in and out of the location is far easier when there are only a handful of people.

I know it's exciting to have all your friends around to watch, and people willing to work for free, but please consider my advice and draw the line someplace. If a person isn't actually doing something useful, get rid of them. Or select certain days on the schedule when they could be useful and tell them to stay home on days that aren't.

STEVE BALDERSON

JUST LIKE COOKING

Casting and crewing a movie might be the most challenging aspect of making a movie, and one that many directors and producers should reevaluate. By casting and crewing your movie correctly, you can avoid having conflicts on the set, maintain a healthy atmosphere, and construct a positive environment in which everyone can thrive.

When I'm casting or crewing a movie, I think of it like cooking. The movie is the dish we're about to make, and each element that goes into making that dish becomes an ingredient. Different locations, props, costumes, and people, each have their own unique color, flavor, energy, and thus each is a unique ingredient. Like saffron, ginger, or cucumber.

I think it's very important to make sure that all the ingredients work well together, both on screen and off. If everyone enjoys being around each other, the atmosphere will be free of conflict. And if any conflict arises, people who enjoy each other tend to handle conflict in a healthy, mature way.

So, think of people like food. Try it. Go on.

Pick someone you know and imagine what kind of ingredient would they be. Are they volatile, or spicy, like, say, cayenne? Are they sweet and rounded, and ordinary, like, say, a Granny Smith apple? Would you pair them up together in the same recipe? And if so, how would you do it? What other ingredients would be needed in order to find the right balance? If you picked the Granny Smith apple person, is there another contender who embodies an ingredient that might work better?

Sometimes this is very difficult to explain to other producers, actors, and directors. Especially those who have been programmed into doing it the traditional way. But, I assure you, this works. It's about understanding chemistry and understanding a person. It's possible even to understand it, and use this process, without ever being in the same room with the person. It's also a very handy tool to use when casting people together that need certain chemistry.

Some people use astrology in a similar way. This process might be stereotyping in one sense, but if it works for you, who cares? The goal is to cast and crew a movie, and to end up with a group of people who get along and shine together on screen.

Even if a person is the best in their field, or the greatest performer, they might not be right for the particular dish you're assembling. It's incredibly important to select the right combination of people to create the ideal environment off screen as much as on screen. When people are spending so much time together in such close proximity to each other, it is imperative that each personality work well together. Each ingredient matters.

Would you rather be working for three weeks with a bunch of talented people who hate each other, or a bunch of talented people who enjoy each other?

In addition to exploring a candidate's skills and talent, it's also a good idea to find out how they see the world and interact with others. How their unique ingredient might give flavor to the ultimate dish.

Ponder your own combinations.

Figs go well on their own, with fresh crisp foods, and even meat but I wouldn't eat a bulb of garlic at the same time. Some might, though. That's fine.

Got a fresh peach, or a plum, and a bossy steak? Try them together, the fruit works surprisingly well on top of the steak.

Roasted beets taste like sweet corn, which is also great with arugula. But I'd avoid pairing them up with gummy worms.

Traditionally, when casting a movie, there are a few standard approaches to how to do it. One is to have an actor read "sides." Sides are just a few pages from a scene in the script.

Doing a cold reading from "sides" is totally unfair to the actor and also to the director. I can't expect an actor to walk in off the street without any previous discussion with me and nail it. Sure, sometimes magic happens. But, it's unfair to ask the actor to do that. It would be most beneficial to everyone involved if the actor and the director could speak about the character in question. Actors act. That's what they do. Most of the good ones can play any part you throw at them.

If an actor does a reading that isn't a match with the director's idea of the role, it is totally unfair for the director to judge that actor. How could that actor know what the director is thinking unless the director says so? Actors can be talented, but most are not psychic. They need some *direction* which—oh wait—that's why they call it a Director.

Irresponsible directors will judge an actor in a cold reading based on their ability to perform without any direction. Those are the directors who want actors who can direct themselves, so he/she doesn't have to do any work.

When I'm casting something, sometimes I don't even work off the script, I just ask the actor to channel the energy inside the character and make it totally improvisational. I explain to each performer that there is no right or wrong way to interpret the character. Part of the exercise is just curiosity. To find out what magic might happen.

Sometimes I'll ask an actor to do two videos, each with a different character. This is a great idea if you've never worked with the individual before. Because, they will show you what kind of an actor they are and you won't have to guess. If the actor shows you two totally different performances, it is clear they have a range and can do a variety of roles. Sometimes, the actor performs both parts in the same way, which suggests a narrower range. Which isn't bad.

Once I had a gal do two video auditions for two roles, and she was pretty much the same in both. Even though they were vastly different characters. But she was great at doing the thing she did. So, I cast her in a part totally suited for that kind of performance. And, she nailed it.

Doing video auditions is also very valuable when you're shooting a film across the globe. When I shot my film *Culture Shock* in London and Paris, the only way for me to audition people was via Skype and video. There was no money to fly overseas to do the traditional casting process.

Traditionalists scoff at my concepts, but I think they work wonders and save lots of time and money. So next time you prepare a casting or audition, think about what it is you want to achieve from it. And do whatever you can to reach the goal.

MAKE IT REWARDING

There might be only a few reasons an actor will want to work for deferred pay. One is about whom they're working with (who are their co-stars, who is directing, and so on). Another might be the type of role. Will the character showcase their talent, or is it a challenging type of role they've never tried before?

When I'm asking someone to work for deferred, I know what I'm asking. I put myself in their shoes and ask, "Would I want to do this project under these circumstances?" I have to be able to answer YES to that question, and if I can't, I won't ask it of someone else.

For $10,000 a day I can tolerate crappy food and miserable conditions. Most everyone else can, too. But what if there isn't that kind of money? If you can't afford to pay people very well, how else can you shape the experience to make it rewarding in other ways? What kinds of things would you need in exchange for money? How can you make it enjoyable? Maybe with really superb food, or a fabulous location and a great working environment? These are the kinds of special cares I think about when putting a movie together.

In addition to making sure my cast connects, and giving each juicy roles to showcase their talent, I make the entire experience a cross between a vacation and summer camp. If you make it so they never want to leave, it's possible that when the opportunity comes up again, *they'd pay you* for the privilege to experience it all over again.

It doesn't have to be an ideal vacation spot like Hawaii. It could be an adventure in other ways. My film *Culture Shock*, which was shot in London, had a daytrip to Paris to see the Eiffel Tower. Filming a movie in London was more than enough, but that added day trip to Paris for a scene that only took an hour to film, was the cherry on top.

You don't have to take your cast and crew to Hong Kong (like I did), or Italy (I'm working on that one), or Hawaii (wouldn't that be lovely?), but please take the time to think about what kinds of things can be added to boost the whole experience during working hours—and after.

When I filmed *Firecracker* in my own backyard, cast and crew from the coasts found Wamego, Kansas exotic. They hadn't had an experience of being in a down-home old-time version of Americana.

The days must be light and enjoyable. People must be allowed to get plenty of sleep. There cannot be anyone negative on the set. All actors and crew people are carefully hand-picked based on more than their abilities (consider their personality and behavior also). The meals must be delicious, activities enjoyable and camaraderie wonderful.

If you can deliver these kinds of things, and make your film shoots a totally rewarding experience for everyone involved, you'll have no problems finding people to work for next to nothing. And you'll probably have them coming back for more.

TAKE THAT HAT OFF

To exist in The Industry where specialists reign, one must be the best they can be at *one* thing. This is how it is in Hollywood, or at least major cities across the globe. If you want to be a DP, or script supervisor, or line producer, or gaffer, and live in a major city, chances are the only way you'll be able to do it for a living is by being a specialist. This means that as you work and learn, you become very good at the *one* thing you know everything about. And because of this, you'll have no idea about anything else.

To exist in the rest of the world, to be an independent filmmaker, one must wear multiple hats and be *many* different things. One day the line producer is also the gaffer, and maybe the next day the script supervisor is a camera assistant. By having your crew wear multiple hats, it can save a lot of time and money. Unless you're making a studio movie, no one needs 50 people on their crew. I don't see any reason to have more than 10. I prefer to keep that number under eight, but on occasion and depending on the shoot, I can see where 12 or 15 might be nice.

Trouble might occur if you bring a specialist into a project designed for people to wear multiple hats. The specialist will struggle with this, and the majority of the time this person will either be horrible to work with, or cause friction on the set.

Of course, some specialists can do different things, but my advice is to make sure these things are talked about before you start filming. Once I had a guy from Los Angeles on my crew who refused to do anything except the activities in his job title. There could be a sudden downpour, people rushing to get the equipment covered and inside to safety, and he'd just stand around and watch everybody. Why didn't he help out? Well, he'd say, "I'm a focus puller. Carrying equipment isn't my job."

Yes, sometimes specialists can come off being total jerks. Which is why I prefer to hire aspiring filmmakers who have little to no experience.

Aspiring filmmakers or interns tend to work harder and have more passion. They are also moldable, agreeable, and excited about all the aspects of movie making. When someone is excited about learning, and thrilled to experience different things, the environment is always enjoyable.

If you do end up hiring an intern or aspiring filmmaker with little experience, be sure to show them how to do different things. Teach them and make it enjoyable for them. One day have them work in the art department, another day have them work with the camera, and the next day in production sound. This way, they will leave your shoot a bit more knowledgeable about filmmaking. It's also possible they'll learn more on your shoot than they would spending thousands of dollars on tuition at a film school. They may not understand the value of their experience immediately, but later they'll be very thankful.

A COLLABORATIVE... ART?

Filmmaking is *not* a collaborative art. It is a collaborative PROCESS. If you're hearing this for the first time, it might seem shocking, but let me explain.

This goes across the board with any artistic endeavor, be it music, painting, or design. Let's use painting as the example. One person can stretch the canvas, another person can mix the paint, but when it comes time, only one person can hold the brush—or it will look like it. If more than one person holds the brush the painting will lack unity and the perspective will be off. Then, of course, you can have another person sell the painting to a gallery, and yet another person at that gallery selling it to the consumer. So, the PROCESS is certainly collaborative.

Sure, filmmaking by committee exists, and I have no problem with filmmaking by committee. People might confuse filmmaking by committee as a collaborate art—it isn't. It's a collaborative process. There always needs to be one person in charge—the head honcho—whether the director, a producer, or a studio executive. If you have too many people making decisions, the end result will be chaotic and lack any kind of unity or focus. Which sometimes happens, and we've all seen examples of the outcome.

When you're about to make a film it's very important to define who is the leader. If you are merely a director who is translating what the producer tells you to do, you need to have a clear understanding of what that means. And so does the producer. You don't want to wait until halfway into your shoot to realize you've done it all wrong, that he's in charge and you aren't.

Once I was working with a make-up person who wouldn't create the "faces" and looks I wanted, but rather, wanted to do it his way. He said, "but this is my art." I replied, "No it isn't. This is about PROCESS. It is your job to use your abilities to translate what I want, because this is my vision, *my* Individual Perspective." If we had our actors wear the make-up he wanted them to wear, the movie would've looked like a cartoon. He had been hired based on his technical skill, not his taste.

On the flip side, there are artists I've worked with that have an absolutely keen eye. When we filmed *The Casserole Club*, I asked Jane Wiedlin to be my second set of eyes. I value her opinion as an artist, and in this case, we had reached an aesthetic understanding of what we were creating, so I knew that if she had any ideas, they would be worth considering. And they were. Still, she knew I was in charge, but I gave her the freedom to speak up if she had an idea that could make the scene brighter, or point out something that didn't seem right, or props that weren't historically accurate.

As a director, if you can define your vision and share those definitions with people, chances are that when you set your crew free to work inside that spectrum, they will create something you love. I usually like to make a list of rules that apply to every aspect of the process. I make a "look book" that illustrates what we're

82

going for. If you tell someone to make it "exotic" or "gothic" and not much else, they could come back with something appropriate for a Tim Burton movie, or at the other end of the spectrum, a look suitable for a slasher film. Neither of which may be what you want. But, it isn't their fault. It is your fault. Because you did not communicate effectively. Remember what I wrote earlier about the meaning of communication being what the *other* person hears—not what you say.

It's very important to illustrate verbally, visually, and in great detail, what it is you're creating so that everyone's on the same page. Then, the collaborative process can be an enjoyable one. But, remember, there must always be one person holding the brush and it's important to define who that is right at the start.

STEVE BALDERSON

STORYBOARDS

You don't need to have elaborately sketched storyboards in full color with photo realistic details, but it is a good idea to have something planned and sketched.

I knew instinctively to sketch storyboards before I knew how important it is. A lot of filmmakers have used this practice throughout history. Hitchcock is well-known for his storyboards— which were elaborately crafted and stunning works of art in their own right.

I spent weeks drawing the storyboards for my film *Firecracker*, and I crafted them with elaborate details. Partly because I wanted to communicate to the actors and crew exactly what each frame would look like. When you are communicating something visually, it's very important to show what it is you're saying, in addition to saying it verbally. Just saying we'll shoot a "close up on that actress" can mean virtually endless options, taken from any angle, anywhere. Do you mean profile, back of the head, face, three quarter turn? Draw it. Then we'll know what you mean.

Again, your storyboards don't have to be pretty. It helps when they are, but the purpose of a storyboard isn't much different than a screenplay. They are merely means to communicate to whomever you are showing what you're about to do. Sometimes, they aren't meant to be shown to anyone.

When I draw storyboards, they're primarily for me and my DP to use as a reference and not really anyone else. Of course, if someone wants to see them, I share them happily. But the sole purpose is so that when I get to the set, I know exactly what I need to shoot, where, and how.

They can be stick figures, crappy drawings, anything. It doesn't matter. Are you making fancy cartoons and publishing high-quality graphic novels? No, you're making storyboards for your movie. Keep the purpose in check.

When I'm sketching storyboards for a scene, I plan on sketches for an entire scene taking up only one sheet of paper. I write the scene number on the top of each page, and once the Master Plan is complete, I can organize the pages of storyboard sheets behind each day of the schedule. So all my shots are there for quick reference each day.

Dennis Hopper and I talked about this at length in his living room. He felt that making storyboards was a great way to plan the vision of a scene, but that once you got on the set and the characters came to life, sometimes it could hurt to rely so coldly on the storyboards. Especially if there was some kind of magic happening outside of the planning. I agreed.

It's a very good idea to do storyboards, even if you never refer to them. Say you're up until three o'clock in the morning dealing with a diva actor who needs babying, and you get little sleep, and the next day you arrive on set feeling like a zombie and have no idea what to do. This has never happened to me, but it has happened to a lot of filmmakers I know. If that were to happen, so long as you were prepared and organized, you'll be able to make it through your day on autopilot. My advice is sketch or plan something, even if it's the bare minimum.

Also allow yourself the freedom to capture something you hadn't thought of before. Actors will do certain things that inspire new shots, new angles. If you get to the set and are inspired by the lighting, or architecture, or atmosphere, it's all right to scrap the planned storyboards and capture something new and in-the-moment.

STEVE BALDERSON

PRODUCT PLACEMENT

Unless you're a famous person making a movie with another famous person, a movie that will be released in cinemas around the planet, chances are you won't find a company willing to PAY YOU to showcase their products or brand name.

Fresh off of *Super Size Me*, Morgan Spurlock directed *The Greatest Movie Ever Sold*, which, after a promise from POM (makers of 100% Pomegranate Juice) to pay $1,000,000 USD, the title became, *POM Wonderful Presents: The Greatest Movie Ever Sold*. You might not be Morgan Spurlock, but there are ways to get sponsors to donate goods and services that will help your production save certain expenses.

During the filming of *Firecracker* the company Red Bull provided the cast and crew with cases of the energy drink to use while shooting.

When I set off to London for the filming of *Culture Shock*, I used product placement as a means to trade services we would otherwise have had to pay for. The two most expensive elements of making a movie are lodging and feeding people.

I emailed every hotel in London asking them for free rooms in exchange for promoting their brand in the film. There would even be scenes filmed in their lobby and guest rooms. Emailing every hotel in London is an easy thing to do but it is incredibly time consuming. There are over 1,000 hotels in London.

First, I went to TripAdvisor to get the list of the most popular places to stay, and then I visited each hotel's individual website to locate their marketing, sales or PR department. Then, I made a spreadsheet in Excel of the people I needed to contact, and their telephone numbers and email addresses. Once I was finished gathering data, I emailed every single one of them.

I heard back from three who were interested. I received half a dozen declines, but other than that, none of the remaining 900+ hotels responded to my request. Nonetheless, I had three! So I began to do more research into each hotel, where each hotel was located (near to an underground stop which would be convenient), what did they look like (cinematographically speaking) and how easy would they be to work with. I chose the best one by far, and once we had lodging taken care of, I went on about food.

I made a "Meal Sponsors Sign Up Sheet" which I passed around to the cast and crew and asked if there were any meals they would like to donate. It's fun for the host to be able to share their favorite cuisine, and also fun for the cast and crew to eat dinner in someone's home—to really experience the culture of where you are and who you're working with.

Another part of product placement is what I would call a "perk." Items that won't necessarily help you shave expenses from the cost of the film but increase morale and give the cast and crew something to enjoy.

Samsonite donated some luggage for us to use as props in the film. We would've used our own luggage, naturally, but having some cool Samsonite pieces really boosted the feeling on set.

Larabar, the makers of the popular heath snack, sent cases of various styles for us to enjoy as a healthy alternative to craft service. And if we couldn't find a meal sponsor, we'd just eat a Larabar! In exchange, I wrote some dialogue in the film to help promote their brand.

There are numerous items in any script suitable for a product placement trade. Make a list of any props you need to get and start calling around to see what kinds of stuff you can get donated. In addition to fun stuff, like luggage or wine, think about practical things too: paper towels, shampoo, and toothpaste. Everyone uses those items every day, and if you don't have to buy them, you'll save money in a variety of areas.

Getting product placement is a time-consuming task. Be prepared to send hundreds of emails and make dozens of calls, most of which will never reply. And most people will reply and decline. Whenever someone replies and agrees, and sends you a lovely case of wine, or donates rooms for you and your cast and crew in a luxury five-star hotel in Europe... you'll find that the time and effort it takes to do this is totally worth it.

ON THE CLOCK

You do not need any fancy, expensive, or magic movie making software to schedule a movie. You simply need some note cards, scotch tape, and Microsoft Word.

To begin the scheduling process, buy a stack of colored note cards.

Each note card will represent a scene from your script. Use yellow cards for all exterior "day" scenes, green cards for interior "day" scenes, blue for inside "night" scenes, and purple for outside "night" scenes.

To make a card, match the card color to the scene in your script. Is it inside, outside, day or night?

On the top of each note card, write in the scene number and title. Then write a brief description of the scene. On the right, list the characters in that scene, and at the bottom, any special props or unique elements (such as a car, animal, or special effects). Then, at the top right corner, put the amount of time you think it will take to shoot that scene.

How long will it take you to shoot the scene? That's up to you.

Think about it from the standpoint of shooting difficulty. Is it a scene filled with action and multiple shots? Maybe you'll want to give yourself extra time. Or, maybe it's a one camera set up but two pages of dialogue that you think you'd be able to do in less than an hour.

I average an hour of shooting time per one page of the script. So, if my scene is two pages long, I'll write down "2 hrs" at the top of the note card. If it's half a page, I'll write down "30 mins."

Then, once I have all the note cards made up for each scene in the entire script, I will separate them into piles based on location. All the scenes/cards to be filmed at The Restaurant in one pile, all the cards for Hotel Room in another. And so forth.

Once you've separated the cards into location piles, you can begin organizing them into "shooting days."

To do this, lay the cards on the table and count the hours. I try to keep the shooting times each day right around eight hours total. (Later, when you add in breaks, travel time, lunches and dinners, you'll see that eight hours shooting time is plenty; more than eight shooting hours makes for a long day. On the flipside, six or seven filming hours is a nice solid yet enjoyable workday.

If your locations have shorter shooting hours (perhaps you have just two cards for the Hotel which add up to three shooting hours), set those aside. Either that day at the hotel will be very light, or you'll match it up with another location and have a "production move" mid-day.

When you've finished organizing the cards, lightly tape the cards together on the reverse side (so if you need to move cards around later on, you won't tear off the front).

Then, tape the strips of days up on your wall.

Each vertical strip of cards represents one shooting day. At the top of each strip I put a pink card that says the location. If you are doing a feature and organizing scenes based on roughly an hour's shoot time per page, you should have somewhere between 12 and 18 days, give or take. Of course, that can be shorter if you aren't changing locations, or longer, if, say, half of your movie takes place in Hong Kong (you'll add a few days travel time just flying there and settling in).

Feel free to rearrange the strips of "days" until you are comfortable with the order of locations. I always try and select an easy location to start, as the first day on set is always the one that should be the lightest.

I keep the note cards taped to a wall in the office during the entire pre-production process. The more you see it, the more familiar you become with each shooting day, and the more comfortable you will be when it comes time to shoot.

Now, we'll incorporate that information into Word, ending up with a shooting schedule, or as I like calling it, the Master Plan.

I've built a template in Word (you'll find it in the Appendix) so that each shooting day fits nicely on a single page. At the top, you'll write in Day One, Day Two, Day Three, and so on, and work on building the entire schedule before you actually pick a date on the calendar. This practice also allows for easy swapping of days, say, if you want to move Day Three to Day Eight, and so forth.

Also in the Appendix is an actual page from the Master Plan (what I call my evolved shooting schedule) detailing the first day of filming *Culture Shock* in London.

It was the first day of principal photography, so I wanted to keep it light. Even though there were only five cards in the strip for this day, there were several location changes and some travel time on the London Underground to take into consideration.

The information at the top is where you will find what actors are needed when, and where they need to show up. I also list crew to the right, so I know which days we'll have extra help.

The first column is for the time on the clock. I've separated it into 15-minute intervals because it's the most efficient. The second column is where the scene numbers go. The third column is for scene name, description, travel directions, addresses, eating venues, bathroom breaks, and so on. Leaving the final column as a place to write what characters are in what scene.

Organizing the Master Plan this way eliminates the need for a Second AD, since the pages in the Master Plan replace the traditional Call Sheets that most actors and crew are familiar with. The Master Plan is much easier to read and understand than traditional Call Sheets.

What happens when your schedule gets wacky? Well, if it does, use a ball point pen, or pencil, and make changes as needed. Usually, if you do a good job organizing the time on the note cards in Step One, and you and your DP modified it ahead of time, and have accounted realistically for travel and break times, it is likely you'll remain on schedule. Or even ahead of schedule.

Once you've made your Master Plan, get out a calendar. Pick the date you want to start shooting, and then all the pages can be renamed from Day One, etc., to a specific day and date. When this is complete, you can send the Master Plan to your cast and crew. I make sure everyone involved has a copy. Each person can use it as a reference to know which days they will be working, or not, or when to plan for a heavy day, or when to let loose on a light one.

Being organized is the most efficient way to make a movie. If the entire cast and crew always know what is supposed to be happening, and at what time, it will help keep everyone on schedule and each day moving swiftly.

If you've worked on a film set, you know how important it is to remain on schedule. The art of scheduling a movie accurately is really one of the most important parts of the filmmaking process.

In order to schedule a movie, clear communication needs to take place between the crew and cast who will shape it. Some DPs will want to spend hours lighting "that shot" while some actors want another hour to prep for the scene. When that happens, you're soon to be behind schedule.

The first thing I do is limit the DP set up time. If he or she has truly given it some thought, there will be an easy way to light nearly any scene in less than 15-30 minutes. On any given budget. But it takes the self-discipline to be able to sit down and plan it. If you wait to decide what to do until you show up on the set, you won't know what you're doing until you get there. In that case, you will not be prepared, and it could take a long time before the camera team is ready to get the shot. Additionally, if the DP has an amazing idea for a shot that requires a long set-up time, communicate about it during the scheduling process and you can mutually agree on a set-up time to put into the Master Plan.

Another thing I do whenever possible is tell my actors to show up "make-up and hair ready." In some cases, I have hired a hair and make-up person, but I tell them to oversee their own schedule. And if Hillary needs to be camera ready at 3pm, she should be on set at 3pm. It is the responsibility of the make-up artist and Hillary to make sure this happens.

I understand that everyone wants to look his or her best whether it's in front of, or behind, the camera. The DP wants the best lighting, the actors want to look their best, the props, costumes, all of it. Each person wants to achieve their best. And I think that's great! When I'm directing something, I want it to be the best possible experience for the viewer. So, I totally understand everyone wanting to be and do his or her best.

What I do not understand is how few people are really willing to take responsibility for themselves to make sure they achieve their goals. I sketch storyboards before showing up on the set. There is no reason the DP can't look at them and design his lighting plan in advance. There is no reason the actors can't look at those plans and know which side of their face will be seen.

I made my storyboards available to the cast and crew of *Firecracker* and I believe only about four people (out of 42) looked at them. Karen Black was one of them. She loved my attention to detail. There was only one moment while we were filming Karen voiced her opinion that she didn't like where I was putting the camera. I simply told her that now wasn't the time for that discussion. The time for conversation was all those weeks earlier when we went through each storyboard together.

Since I filmed *Firecracker*, I've never had an unorganized shooting day. And I've never been behind schedule. Even if I've experienced a scene running over the pre-planned time, I average about an hour ahead of the scheduled wrap time each day.

Yes, it is possible to make a feature film wherein you don't have to work 12-14 hours a day. The trick is to check vanity at the door, really communicate with clarity and focus, and work with people who love taking responsibility for themselves.

YOU DON'T NEED TO YELL

I was on a film shoot recently where I wasn't producing or directing, just a fly on the wall. It was really a great experience to observe the daily dynamics of a film set that wasn't my own. I highly encourage everyone who is interested in making movies to visit someone else's set. Whether you are an actor, director, DP, Make-up artist, costumer, writer, etc. It's an incredibly educational experience. No matter if you're a Pro or a total Newbie. And it doesn't matter what kind of a movie it is.

The first film set I visited which wasn't my own was Sean Penn's *The Crossing Guard* starring Jack Nicholson. The second film set I visited was a no budget indie shoot for a first-time director. Each was on the farthest and most opposite ends of the filmmaking spectrum. One had over 100 crew people, endless trucks lining the street, a buffet of craft service that rivaled the best restaurants, while the other had none of that and just a handful of aspiring Production Assistants. It didn't matter though, because both had interesting dynamics to study and learn from. This is why I suggest getting yourself on any film set, anywhere, and just take it all in. Compare how different directors work and how different types of actors work. And do it as many times as you can. It will help you better define how you'd like to operate your own film set.

In all the differences, there was one thing I remembered that I'd totally forgotten about. I forgot because I haven't used one in years. The traditional AD (either a First or Second Assistant Director).

Because I schedule everything ahead of time and manage all the administrative aspects of my shoots, I haven't needed one. I do realize that not everyone is as hyper organized as me, so you might need an AD or two. And when you interview them, my advice is to keep an eye/ear open to how they communicate.

I've never been in a "How to be an AD" workshop, but something about how most of them behave suggests they have learned to be stern, mean-mannered, loud-mouthed, and generally petulant or irritating. It is so totally counterproductive to behave that way in a job position like that of the first or second AD.

I understand it is important to stay on schedule. But there's no reason to yell about it and to push people around like a drill sergeant. All that does is make people disrespect you. Getting what you want is the goal, right? There are two ways to accomplish that: the respectful way and the disrespectful way.

Try this exercise. Ask someone in a soft and friendly tone of voice, "Could you pass the ketchup?" Chances are the other person will likely not think twice, and just pass it. Now, try it on another person and use a firm drill sergeant voice and demand, "Give that to me. *Come on!*" You might end up getting the ketchup, but that person won't like the experience of passing it to you. And afterwards, they will likely hold some resentment for being treated like an inferior person. And if they are continued to be treated that way, those tiny resentments will build up until they become so big that person will leave the set each night and never want to work with you again.

ADs who have been programmed to behave like Nazis will disagree with me, of course. But never mind them. The easiest way to get what you want is to figure out how to avoid conflicts from the beginning. If you schedule correctly before you start shooting, you won't need to worry about staying on schedule. If you communicate with your make-up artist clearly, you'll already know how much time each person will take, and you can plan for it.

If you use archaic ways of scheduling a shoot, just because everybody else does, or "that's the way it's always been done," you'll have an outcome just like everyone else: over budget, behind schedule, etc.

But if you really take everything into consideration from the get-go, you can plan for it all. Then, I suppose, you won't need a professional AD. You could just use an intern who knows how to communicate with people in a clear and respectful way.

I read an article once about the insanity of director David O. Russell humiliating people on set. Included was a letter from George Clooney that I want to share with you. Those of you who watched my *Wamego: Making Movies Anywhere* documentary trilogy saw the clips of him freaking out on Lily Tomlin. I cannot understand why, with all the talented directors out there who are professional and polite, like me for instance, one would continue to hire people who abuse their coworkers.

In 1999, George Clooney got into a fistfight with David O. Russell on the set of *Three Kings*.

Here's what George writes:

He'd throw off his headset and scream, "Today the sound department fucked me!" For me, it came to a head a couple of times. Once, he went after a camera-car driver who I knew from high school. I had nothing to do with his getting his job, but David began yelling and screaming at him and embarrassing him in front of everybody. I told him, "You can yell and scream and even fire him, but what you can't do is humiliate him in front of people. Not on my set, if I have any say about it".

Another time, he screamed at the script supervisor and made her cry. I wrote him a letter and said, "Look, I don't know why you do this. You've written a brilliant script, and I think you're a good director. Let's not have a set like this. I don't like it and I don't work well like this". I'm not one of those actors who likes things in disarray. He read the letter and we started all over again. But later, we were three weeks behind schedule, which puts some pressure on you, and he was in a bad mood. These army kids, who were working as extras, were supposed to tackle us. There were three helicopters in the air and 300 extras on the set. It was a tense time, and a little dangerous, too. David wanted one of the extras to grab me and throw me down. This kid was a little nervous about it, and David walked up to him and grabbed him. He pushed him onto the ground. He kicked him and screamed, "Do you want to be in this fucking movie? Then throw him to the fucking ground!" The second assistant director came up and said, "You don't do that, David. You want them to do something, you tell me". David grabbed his walkie-talkie and threw it on the ground. He screamed, "Shut the fuck up! Fuck you", and the AD goes, "Fuck you! I quit".

He walked off. It was a dangerous time. I'd sent him this letter. I was trying to make things work, so I went over and put my arm around him. I said, "David, it's a big day. But you can't shove, push *or humiliate people who aren't allowed to defend themselves". He turned on me and said, "Why don't you just worry about your fucked-up act? You're being a dick. You want to hit me? You want to hit me? Come on, pussy, hit me". I'm looking at him like he's out of his mind. Then, he started banging me on the head with his head. He goes, "Hit me, you pussy. Hit me". Then, he got me by the throat and I went nuts. Waldo, my buddy, one of the boys, grabbed me by the waist to get me to let go of him. I had him by the throat. I was going to kill him. Kill him. Finally, he apologized, but I walked away. By then, the Warner Bros. guys were freaking out. David sort of pouted through the rest of the shoot and we finished the movie, but it was truly, without exception, the worst experience of my life.*

—

.

EDITS WIDE SHUT

Another effective way to save time and money is to be aware of editing during each stage of the production process.

The first time I'm aware of editing comes at the beginning, when I'm doing a shot list, or storyboards for the film. I can see in my mind how the scene will be cut together and how the rhythm of the shots will affect the pace of the movie. Of course, some of these ideas will change during the actual filming process. But, overall, I get a really clear sense about what the viewer will experience at this early stage.

If I get the sense that the scene will end on this shot, or that shot, or in a certain moment, I will make a note in the screenplay. Sometimes this means crossing out entire sequences. The screenwriters I've worked with in my career are usually fine with this, but I can understand how sometimes screenwriters might react in a negative way. My advice: just don't tell them. You could also have an agreement in place about who has the creative control.

If I know I'm not going to use a particular shot in the final movie, why bother wasting the time or money on the set by filming it?

Perhaps not every person who considers himself or herself a director can imagine this ahead of time. I'd suggest that if you can't foresee what the viewer will be going through, you might want to consider finding another job. Isn't that the whole point of being the director? In that case, perhaps you should turn your attention to working in another aspect of filmmaking, or perhaps take up film criticism professionally.

Being involved in the editing process is the easiest way to get the hang of rhythm, timing, and pacing. Every director should be his or her own film editor at least during one phase of the editing process. It's okay to have help on technical matters, and to bring in additional editors for multiple points of view, but the director should know when to stop the scene, where to make the cut. Having that knowledge will help shape the way you write and film your movies.

Back to the set. There was a scene in my film *Occupying Ed* where Holly Hinton and Christopher Sams are lying on the floor playing chess. There's a great subtle dolly move inching closer and closer to them throughout the scene. When the dolly stops, she calls out checkmate, and that's where the scene ends.

However, in the screenplay the scene continued. There was another page of dialogue and a couple of jokes. I didn't think the jokes were funny, even though everyone else on set disagreed with me. I thought about filming the rest of the scene in order to test this later. But, I decided to *not* film them, and to just end the scene at checkmate. It felt right. I knew that even had we filmed the rest of the scene as it was written, I'd be cutting it out in the editing room. It made no sense to waste the next hour shooting the rest of the scene when I knew it wouldn't make it into the film. I decided it was best to just go on to the next shot, the next scene.

If you've only made a couple of movies, and aren't confident yet you can do this, my advice is to go ahead and shoot the scene as it's written and decide later. After you've made more than a dozen movies it'll become second nature, and you'll feel great about saving the time and money on set.

STEVE BALDERSON

FILM WEATHER

Unless I'm on a beach wading in perfectly clear seawater, the ideal temperature for me to experience is a non-humid 70 degrees F (that's 21C for everyone else on the planet except the USA). I keep interior temps at 70F all year long. I sleep better, think better, and create better. There are times when I can't control the climate. Before scheduling a movie shoot, it's always a great idea to consider where you're going to shoot and what the temperature will be.

Dennis Hopper once told me it's better to shoot in sweltering heat than it is to shoot in bitterly cold. He was right. It wasn't until my first winter shoot that I realized how debilitating it is to shoot a movie in cold weather.

When the temps get cold enough, and the wind chill kicks in, it can be beyond miserable. In addition, it can be dangerous. Frostbite is a concern. It is really hard to operate cameras and things with huge padded gloves. Imagine being an actor, trying to compose yourself and stay in character when your body starts involuntarily shaking. Or what about the blood draining from your face and leaving your nose bright red and cheeks pale? These are problems that one must deal with when shooting in the cold.

There are also some dangers when shooting a movie in the heat. People are at risk for heat stroke and the sort. But, tolerating the temperature impact on your body is manageable. It is easy to provide water to people, make sure everyone stays in the shade whenever possible to avoid heat exhaustion. Sometimes it happens, of course, and usually when the heat index is higher than normal (this is like a wind chill but reverse).

I've filmed many movies in warm temps. My first film *Pep Squad* was produced in Kansas during July and August, which can be very humid and stifling. It was disgusting. Actors experienced their make-up sliding down their faces, and several people on the crew smelled terrible.

Stuck! was even worse. Filmed during early summer in Macon, Georgia, where the humidity is so thick you can cut it and spread it on a piece of toast. The location where we filmed the jail cells was on the second floor of a building with no air conditioning. The owners refused to open the windows at night to cool it down for us. So we were forced to work in miserable conditions. Visually it looked great: everyone was a little shiny with sweat and the contrast shooting in B&W worked out in our favor.

During *The Casserole Club* we filmed during the late summer in Palm Springs, and I made sure the air conditioning ran throughout the shoot. Some people have the belief you should shut all the appliances off or turn off the AC when you shoot. That makes no sense to me because you'll just add room noise back in later. It's super easy to match the frequency of the room noise and air conditioner and remove it later. Maybe back in the day this was more challenging. Anyway, I've never worried about shutting off the AC or Heat. Or unplugging the fridge.

Likewise, think about other factors such as: is it hurricane season? Tornado season? Rainy season? Dry season? Allergy season? How many hours of daylight versus night will you have? In real life, it would always be ideal to live and work in an environment steady at 70F. All things to think about when scheduling your next movie.

DIRECTING SEX SCENES

Some people say there's nothing sexy about filming a sex scene. I'd like to say that's mostly true, but the truth is, sometimes they can be incredibly sexy. One of the secrets of filming a sex scene is the same as filming a scene with gruesome violence. Basically, anything that is supposed to be graphic should always follow the rule of *less is more*.

Give the audience something to feel and they will feel it. If you show it to them, they will not feel it. Instead, they will look at it. The more they see, the less they feel. Whereas, if you limit the graphic shots, you will give the audience a visceral reaction to what you're showing them.

In my film *Watch Out* there is a scene in the end where we had to film some toes being cut off of actress and bestselling author Jillian Lauren. The only reason this scene works is because the graphic visuals are kept to a precise minimum. There are three short moments when we see something graphic in that scene, and each shot is less than a second. The sound effects create something so gross and violent that the audience isn't really conscious of the fact that they are, in fact, not seeing much of anything.

The best sex scenes are done in the same way. The more you hear breathing, see shots of skin in the shadows, avoiding the explicit, the more erotic it will be.

Another secret to sex scenes is to involve the actors. Ask them what parts of their bodies they are comfortable with showing, and what parts they are not. Most people know their own bodies well enough to tell you from what angle certain shapes or features are accentuated, and which angles to avoid.

If you can bring your actors into the creation of the sex scene (or a graphically violent scene), they will also be more comfortable in the process of filming it. It is also a good idea to keep them as relaxed as possible or else it will show on screen. Unless the intent is to show nervousness, in which case, it might be useful to not involve them in order to accentuate their nervousness.

If you're doing a sex scene with a woman who loves her breasts but hates the way her butt looks, or a guy who loves his ass but doesn't think his abs are good enough, it can be really fun to use these obstacles as fuel to inspire your storyboards and shot list. Don't think about them as obstacles, but rather, an exciting experiment in creation. How can you storyboard a list of shots that gives the actors what they want, and also the audience what they want, without compromising either side? I love challenges like this.

It's also a good idea to have a closed set when doing any kind of graphic scene. There is no reason for every person to be present. You only need the DP, the director and the sound guy. Maybe the Make-Up and Hair person. Gaffers and Grips, Assistants and the like, can easily step outside for the take and return immediately after the shot. The less people present, the more comfortable the actors will be and the better the scene will be.

CONTINUITY

Face it. The only people who care about continuity are people who care about continuity. The majority of people watching a movie don't think about it at all. Instead, they're watching the movie. People who care about continuity are not watching the movie—they're watching props and costumes.

It's okay to encourage people making the movie to be aware of continuity, but there's no reason to be obsessive over it. Your actors usually look the same in the morning as they do a couple hours later, do they not? Unless you're shooting a scene that will take three days to film, it really shouldn't be that big of a deal.

In ancient times, it did take the studios three full days to shoot a single scene. So, it was important to make sure the costumes and hairdos looked the same, since in the final movie the scene might only be 90 seconds long. And if there were drastic changes in such short timeframe, it would be visually jarring to the audience. But those days are long gone. Now it just takes a few hours to shoot a scene.

There are still people who obsess over continuity. I'm here to tell you that unless it's a really stupid mistake, it doesn't matter. The viewer will still watch, and continue watching, until they have to get up and go to the loo.

Imagine a scene where a woman is wearing red as she climbs into a car. The car speeds away. In the next shot, the car stops, she gets out, and is wearing blue.

People obsessed over continuity will go on and on about that being a horrible mistake. Whereas any normal person can see she's obviously changed clothes, so it must be a different time or different day. Oftentimes directors, or costumers, will use a change of clothes as an unconscious suggestion that time has passed. There is no continuity error there. Just an error in the eyes of the person obsessed with continuity.

Sometimes I like to dress my actors in the same costume throughout the entire movie. Have a look at *Culture Shock*. With the exception of a few scenes, all the actors are wearing the same things throughout. I used the children's cartoon *Scooby Doo* as the aesthetic template. Daphne, for example, always wears that purple dress and lime-green scarf. Velma is always in that hideous Orange sweater. Shaggy is always in that green shirt. Yet, has any person watching the show ever stopped and said, "Wait a minute. She was wearing that yesterday. Obviously must have been out all night. What a slut." No. No one says that.

Aside from being a fun artistic choice to dress your actors in the same costume for the entire film, it eliminates the need for a costume person. The actors can just take care of their clothes themselves! If you decide to do that, be sure to bring enough Fabreeze, or buy two identical outfits, because your actor will stink after wearing the same outfit five days in a row.

BE STRATEGIC, PATIENT

I know when you're filming your movie, you're excited and want to share that excitement with your friends on various social networks. But hesitate. Think twice about posting photos too soon. Movies take a long time to complete, and in this world of "now, now, now" you might be shooting yourself in the foot by posting things prematurely.

Think of it backwards. When your movie is about to premiere at a festival, you will want to publicize it and get people to go see it. Naturally, you'll want a website and a press kit, photos and such, and a trailer for people to see. This will get them excited about the film and hopefully they will want to see it. I would suggest launching the trailer for your movie about a month prior to that first screening.

Backing up from there, a month or so before that trailer launch, you will want some kind of web presence to showcase some photos and information for festivals. Maybe you'll already have a trailer. My advice is to keep it hidden from the general public. A password protected Vimeo or unlisted YouTube page work well.

Before you can submit your movie to festivals, buyers and critics, you'll have to complete the final sound mix, score it, and do the color timing. All of those things take time. Some of those can be done quicker than others if you pay top dollar. If you're paying less, it might take four to five times longer to complete post-production.

Think of it from the audience's point of view. When you see a trailer for a movie, and it says "coming soon" at the end, do you expect that to be in a few weeks, a few months, or a couple years? Ask yourself if it's a year later, will you still be interested in seeing that movie? Will you even remember it?

It's very important to tell your actors, crew, and friends, that when you're filming your project, it might be the best idea to wait and not post any photos or news about the film until after it's totally complete.

That first premiere screening very well might be—at the earliest—an entire calendar year away. And most likely the release of that project will be the year after that.

I made this mistake when promoting my film *Firecracker*. We filmed it in 2003 and couldn't find distribution for a long time. I had to invent a way to keep hooking the audience that was already generated, to keep them interested until it came out. So, first I made a behind-the-scenes documentary (*Wamego: Making Movies Anywhere*). I released that and used it as a promotional tool for the film, without any spoilers.

Firecracker is based on a true story, so I gathered up all my research and figured out a way to showcase bits of information on a monthly basis via a "True Story Investigation" section of the website. This would help pacify the fans who were there already, and would also hook new ones. Without those monthly updates, we likely would've started to lose our audience.

It was fun to do all that, but it was a full-time job. It is much easier to be strategic with your marketing and wait until the movie will be ready for people to see. If you tell them about it too soon, you might lose them by the time it's released.

So take all the photos you want, and make all the behind the scenes clips you can! But, just be careful about making them public too soon. Because coming up with a really great idea to maintain awareness of your project to last the next two years can be tough.

There are different kinds of publicity meant for different stages of making a movie and releasing it.

The most important is the publicity to sell the movie to the audience. This is done once the film has *already* been sold or licensed to a distribution company, and although that distribution company will have its own PR and marketing plan, chances are the attention to your title won't be as much as you can do on your own (or with another hired PR firm).

During this phase of publicity, you'll want to get out there on social media and be featured in magazines geared towards your demographic (if you have a tattoo themed movie, for instance, you'll want to hit up all the magazines and news outlets for ink and body modification). You'll also want to get your movie reviewed by all the critics you can—no matter what media outlets they write for.

Please make note that it can be counterproductive to do this kind of publicity unless you have a release date. Most media outlets do not want to publish a story that isn't newsworthy. If your film doesn't have a release date, or hasn't been picked up for distribution yet, it doesn't matter to the general populace. If the public has no means to see your film, why would anyone want to read about it?

It could also be counterproductive because in our culture of instant gratification, when someone reads about something they are interested in, they want to click on it *now* and buy it *now* or watch it *now*. It's one thing to build buzz for your project a few weeks from the release date, but it's another thing to try and build it over the course of a year. People will lose interest unless you can hook them and keep them hooked.

The second most important publicity is the kind to use as a means to get distribution. This kind of marketing can sometimes overlap with marketing to the general public. Be careful. You'll want to get some advance reviews, share news about film festival screenings and acclaim or awards won, but remember what I previously mentioned: If your film doesn't have a release date, or hasn't been picked up for distribution yet, it doesn't matter to the general populace.

This kind of publicity could be more focused. For example, if your film is going to premiere at a film festival that industry buyers will be attending, you might consider compiling a list of every distribution company acquisitions person and send postcards to alert them. Emails can get buried and lost these days. I've found direct mailing works wonders because most people have forgotten about it. And when they receive a sharply designed, tangible object they can hold, it's unusual. And memorable.

If you want to hire a professional PR firm, be prepared to pay thousands of dollars. They will likely not spend as much time pushing your project as you would on your own, but they know whom to call and have relationships with the media bigwigs you don't. Still, that doesn't keep you from picking up the phone and introducing yourself to those same bigwigs. Remember, emails get lost or buried. It's much more effective to call the Editor of whatever news outlet on the phone directly.

Another thing you might want to do is gather endorsements or quotes about your project from celebrities to use in your press kit. This needs to be done totally under the radar and in private. It's a great idea to include this kind of thing in your marketing materials. It's silly to think that people are mostly incapable of independent thought, but it's really true. If you tell them what to think of your movie, they generally do. And if so-and-so said it was great, well, then, it must be!

Remember that famous tagline: you only have one chance to make a first impression. Premature publicity of any sort could be a disaster, so when you're about to embark on your own marketing journey, ask yourself, "Is now the right time? Could we benefit from waiting a bit longer?"

It always amuses me when actors pretend to get shy around the media. Most of them, even if they deny it, are actors because they love and crave attention. As children, they were the first to jump up in front of a group and "perform."

Many actors are also fairly insecure people. I mean, think about it. They turn their life's objective into avoiding their truest self in exchange for always being somebody else. The good ones get paid for it. Sometimes, actors find out there's very little time left to be themselves, and some might even forget who they used to be altogether.

Actors might also be called professional liars. The good ones are so good at lying, that you actually believe what they're saying and feeling. Even though it's totally fake. I mean, it is a movie, right!? Someone wrote those words for him or her to say. And in some cases, this isn't always exclusive to their performances on screen.

Sometimes the best actors can achieve amazing results in normal day-to-day life.

Anyway, if you're a director or producer and you ever come upon an actor who is shy around the media or afraid to do interviews with the press, you might need to pretend you understand them and hold their hands, but know, deep down, by the time they get into the interview they'll be all lit up, performing, doing what they do best. And they *always* eat it up. You'll see.

Depending on the actor, it may be a good idea to give them a script to follow. Some actors are brilliant at improvisation. But many need a back-story, a character arc and a sheet of dialogue. Or, at least, talking bullet points.

I like to supply my actors with a go-to bullet point list of topics to discuss about our movie. Questions to answer in a precise way, using careful language. Sometimes I'll even include a list of topics to avoid, such as, giving away any plot secrets or proprietary information.

Another idea I've advised other filmmakers in the past, is to be a kind of go-between with the media. Have the interviewer send you the questions first, so you can look over them and make sure there's nothing offensive asked, or anything that might cause the project harm. And, likewise, there might be a question asked the actor would otherwise not know how to answer. If this scenario happens you can tell the actor what to say.

You could also tell the interviewer you'll pass along their email address or phone number to the actor and let the actor take it from there. Whichever way makes you more comfortable. Some of the more famous actors don't like having their email or number given out, so in most cases dealing with a celebrity of any kind, this will be the best avenue to take.

Actors are a funny bunch, and of course I was generalizing their personalities earlier. Not every actor is a ruthless, self-absorbed fame-hungry monster. Some of my greatest friends are amazing actors and their gifts and talents are greatly appreciated. Without actors, there's no such thing as a movie. We need them. And we need to cherish them. But, when it comes time to promote your movie, you might need to nudge them a little bit this way or that.

I think it's fun to investigate and explore existing press kits online. They're easy to find. Making your own isn't really that difficult, but it will take some time.

There are no rules to crafting a good press kit. I've seen incredibly complicated press kits, three-dimensional designs, and short and concise press kits. In ancient times, press kits were usually a package (or folder) with papers inside, photographs, and other bulky things used to promote the product.

These days press kits are usually entirely online or easily shared via email. Some might consist of audio/visual treats and be shared on a flash drive. But most everyone agrees that there's no reason to spend money on something when you can achieve the same result for nothing. So, I say, go with a simple PDF. You don't need to print anything. A link to Vimeo works just great.

First, write a well-formed synopsis. It's often a good idea to include a medium-length synopsis and an even shorter one. Keep in mind that you should make it sound exciting, as if you were writing a review. Most often, journalists are lazy and want to simply copy-n-paste what you've written so they don't have to work so hard. And in the process, when the Boston Globe (or whomever) writes that your movie is a "fast-paced gem" you can easily lift that quote from their article, quote the Boston Globe as saying it, and use it for promoting your movie. Even though you were the one who wrote it. Remember that.

Write biographies for your key cast and crew. If you aren't working with anyone notable in show business, write their bios full of excitement and wonder about the world those people live in. If your lead actress was a former beauty queen, or if your DP was an escaped felon, or if your supporting actor was a hot dog eating champion—share that info! Weird stories make for great media coverage.

You might want to consider incorporating a mock interview with yourself and other key players in your project. Sometimes this acts as a showcase for the type of interesting interview you can do. I like to make up a game of 20 Questions and keep them light and simple, and sometimes juicy and controversial.

Include some stills from your film. Some should be glossy shots of the actors that might be considered a scene from the film, or a portrait. Other shots can be from behind-the-scenes, showing the camera and lighting set-ups, or certain moments while filming is taking place.

You'll definitely want to include a link to the trailer, and maybe even some clips from the film. Some people with online or broadcast capabilities could run clips of your movie during their news segment. (For an example, check out the opening 10-15 minutes of "Wamego: Making Movies Anywhere" which shows news stories about my movie Pep Squad as featured on the nightly news.)

Consider including other reviews or other third-party blurbs. The world is incredibly lazy when it comes to independent thought. By sharing that a dozen (hopefully influential) people love your movie, it sends the signal your movie is great. "Why, if so-and-so loved it, it must be good!"

Keep in mind that at the end of the day, of course you want your project to speak for itself. Sometimes, however, if you don't tell people in the media what they're looking at, they won't know what to think. So even if it sounds a little creepy, or pretentious, you'd better do it. Or you might risk getting lost in the shuffle of all the people who are.

A few years back I was staying at the Bowery Hotel in New York City, having dinner outside the restaurant there. It was a lovely, quiet night in NYC and the food and wine were great. At some point during my meal I noticed a group of men with large cameras congregating nearby on the sidewalk. I didn't think they were there for me, but I was curious why they kept staring at me. Perhaps they thought I was someone else.

Behind me, inside the restaurant, carefully hidden behind the wall, practically sitting in the corner (it had to be uncomfortable) was Cameron Diaz. I took a moment to realize that the experience I was having was far more enjoyable than the one she was having. Imagine it. Cameron Diaz can't sit outside on the street and enjoy a nice dinner in the open air. Unless she wants to be bombarded by paparazzi and mobs of tourists and fans. How sad that must be, to always be cooped up inside places, shoved into the corner so no one can see her. What a limitation.

A while later, one of my movies was having a premiere at the Egyptian Theatre in Hollywood. I received a call from a Public Relations person, who asked if their client could be added to the guest list. Sure, I said. The PR person added that the paparazzi would be alerted to get good photo ops. That surprised me. And, suddenly the world of celebrity became crystal clear. Most of these people were famous for no reason. They were famous because their PR people arranged for it to appear as though they are famous.

Cameron Diaz, obviously, has a reason to be famous. She's appeared in many movies that have been seen by billions of people. There's a reason she's recognized. But, there are a lot of people out there who have no reason at all to be stalked by paparazzi.

Once at LAX, I saw a black suburban drive up and stop. A famous actor got out and walked across the sidewalk to the special entrance of American Airlines. Just before the actor got out of the car, a paparazzi had arrived and was waiting for him. I wondered: how did this paparazzi person know the actor would arrive at precisely 9:26 a.m. for a quick 30-second walk across the pavement? What are the chances? We all know there is no such thing as coincidence. I'm pretty sure the actor's PR person had called someone to ensure that his or her client would be photographed at LAX.

It's true: Hollywood is an illusion. Both on screen and off. Of course, the general public, or Sheeple, have no idea how fabricated it really is. My advice is, if you have something to sell or share with the world... might as well use it.

SOUND MAKES A MOVIE

The sound quality of a movie is the single most important thing to focus on. Audiences will tolerate inferior image quality if the sound is perfect, but they will not tolerate a perfect visual image if the sound is inferior. Naturally, you want to have both the image *and* the sound as perfect as possible, but if you must throw more money into one of these separate jars—pick the sound jar.

When I started out in the business there were specialty sound houses that produced and edited a movie's sound. Even if you had no money, it still cost around $50,000. Of course, back then, we were shooting on film and had to imprint the final sound onto celluloid. Today, since film is obsolete, and almost everyone can download sound editing software, it is possible to get top-level sound quality for a fraction.

I can't remember all their names, but Lisa Hannan and Paul N. J. Ottosson worked at that sound house where I did the post sound on my first film *Pep Squad*. They were both incredibly nice people and also exceptionally talented. I remember telling them I wanted my sound design to rival that of *The Long Kiss Goodnight,* the surprisingly cool yet underrated movie starring Geena Davis. They agreed and their sound work in *Pep Squad* is phenomenal.

Paul and I have continued to work together many times over the years, and he won back-to-back Oscars in Sound for *The Hurt Locker* and again for *Zero Dark Thirty*. He's the best in the business, and the lessons he taught me are immeasurable.

I'll mention one thing he taught me during the post sound in *Watch Out*. There's a hilarious scene with Peter Stickles eating at a Lobster restaurant where the production sound had an echo to it (either because the boom wasn't placed in the right location, or for whatever other reason). On the reverse angle, the production sound of the other character, wasn't echoey at all. Instead of removing the echo from Peter's shots, Paul added more echo to the reverse shot. Matching the echo.

That is one lesson I loved learning, and that never occurred to me before. You don't have to have crystal clear sound, you just need to make sure the sound goes by smoothly, so the audience doesn't get sonically jarred from shot to shot, or scene to scene. I then remembered all the "bugs" and "weather" sounds Paul used in my film *Firecracker*. Instead of removing the cicadas, he added more.

It's about how to take what would normally be considered an error, or a sonic mistake, and using creativity to solve the problem. If you use this way of thinking, and have taken good steps during production to insure you've got at least a good foundation to your sound, you, like me, will never need to do any ADR. I remember Paul telling me that my production sound on *Firecracker* was better quality than the production sound in the blockbuster *Spiderman 2*, which required a ton of ADR, and also for which he was nominated for an Academy Award.

Another trick I learned about sound: if you remove the bass from the dialogue, it's easier to hear. Try this next time you're in your car listening to NPR. Put the bass and treble at equal, listen for a bit, then remove just a small bit of the bass. See what I mean? Or, rather, *hear* what I mean?

It's also fun to play around with Foley. And sometimes the absence of Foley. In *Firecracker* I wanted to have the mother's character (played by Karen Black) make very heavy sounds as she walked—like the gravity in her world was intense. On the flip-side, I wanted to remove all the feet Foley when it came to the carnival world, so when the carnival singer (also played by Karen Black) walked across the room, it was as if she were floating, feet never touching the ground. Of course, this kind of thing is all absorbed subconsciously. Most viewers never notice those kinds of things.

Creating sonic landscapes is just as much fun as creating the visuals. Remember this next time you're watching a movie or making one of your own.

The music and score can also make or break a movie. I've seen a lot of movies that have really crappy soundtracks and music that is, well, just horrible. If you are hunting for a composer to do your score, make sure they are the right person sonically. I mean, they might be a great musician but ask yourself if their particular style of music fits with the tone of your movie.

Johnette Napolitano, the singer from the 1980s band Concrete Blonde, scored my first film *Pep Squad*. I knew she was the right person for the cheeky campy sound I was going for with that film, and she did a haunting vocal version of America the Beautiful she called "Amerika." It was her first film score, and it was fun to work with her on it. I even came up with the idea to incorporate drum cadences, which were recorded by our local high school marching band. Pleasant Gehman was working on a spoken word album with Kristian Hoffman at the time, and Johnette had a recording of Pleasant's "Super Mega Zsa Zsa," and played it for me. As soon as I heard it, I fell head over heels for it. The totally insane part was that when I placed it into the movie, the song fit the scene perfectly, beats actually happening on certain cuts, and ending at exactly the right moment. Total synchronicity.

Different composers have different methods of working. Johnette made several variations of each theme and left me in charge of where to place them in the film. Sometimes musicians scored music to fit an actual scene or sequence with acute attention to detail.

The Enigma had previously made some music with Trent Reznor of Nine Inch Nails, and composed some of the music for the carnival sections of my film *Firecracker*. My dad Clark played all the Chopin Nocturnes you hear in the movie.

Then I met the genius Rob Kleiner. Rob is a Grammy-nominated talent beyond talents, and a great guy who is a total pleasure to be around. Rob scored five of my films including the incomparable score for *Stuck!* Rob's sonic brilliance comes into play as another character in each movie. His music can be subtle or big, but always right in tune and in step with the rhythm and tone of each given film.

I've worked with dozens of other artists who have provided songs for inclusion into different scores. The Woodlands is Samuel and Hannah Robertson, who create absolutely breathtaking stuff. Samuel also made a solo project called Quiet Arrows, which is equally arresting, and a couple of his songs became part of the *Occupying Ed* score, which was composed by Kevin Peirce.

Even if you don't know famous musicians, it is totally possible to find super great music out there. My advice is to keep in mind that the right music will make your movie awesome, and the wrong choices could make it horrible to sit through.

Also keep in mind that just because you like a song, doesn't mean everyone else will. I encourage you to share the music with other people before including it in your movie. Just in case.

EDITING IS FUN

Or, it *can* be. You don't have to make it miserable, or confusing, or tedious. One of the tricks in editing your movie swiftly is similar to my trick on preventing writer's block when you're working on your screenplay:

Keep going.

If you hit a roadblock, or a scene that is troublesome, you're thinking about it too much. The first order of business should be assembling what you've shot. Stop thinking and just lay down the shots. If you refuse to not think, and the scene is troublesome, move on to the next scene. You can always come back to that scene later. The first assembly isn't the final cut. There's no reason to trick yourself into thinking it will be. Trust me, you will make various tweaks multiple times until you're satisfied.

The first thing I do is make sure all my clips are logged and tagged appropriately, with names that are easy to find and read. I'll also make note if a shot is no good, so I don't need to watch it again.

Then I pick a scene, any scene, to start. Sometimes it's at the beginning; sometimes it's about 10 minutes into the film. From there, I will simply assemble each scene as it plays out, in sequential order, until I reach the end. Then, I'll go back and do the first part.

After the First Assembly is complete, I'll go in and inspect each scene on a more detailed level. This is the time to fiddle with cutting frames here and there, making each sequence seamless. This is the time to think about the rhythm of the movie. Don't waste your time trying to do those things when you're simply building the First Assembly. Wait until after the assembly is complete, and then do it.

Once you do that for the whole film, you'll have the Second Assembly. When I have the Second Assembly complete, I will watch it start to finish, making notes as I do. I don't actually make any changes when watching the Second Assembly, I'll just observe what's there. Then, after a complete viewing, I'll go back and implement more changes. Sometimes I'll watch it again at the editing system and make additional changes. But most often, that is the point at which it's time to watch on a TV or away from the computer. Next, you'll have your Rough Cut.

I think it's important to watch the Rough Cut where you normally watch films. Is this on your home laptop? Your TV room? On your iPad? Wherever you normally watch movies is the place to view your Rough Cut. It'll take you out of editing, and into watching it as entertainment. You'll do yourself a great disservice if you only watch the movie in the editing room.

After watching the Rough Cut, make any additional changes, and keep repeating the cycle until you are happy with it. At some point you'll have your Final Cut.

Just keep in mind when you start the editing process that there will be various versions. Your First Assembly is *not* the final cut. It isn't even the Second Assembly. By remembering that, and knowing it, you'll be able to make the First and Second Assembly in no time flat. Which will get you to the Rough Cut sooner than later, and on to the Final Cut enjoyably and efficiently.

The first time I worked with a professional Editor it was a disaster. The guy had failed to connect with the tone and energy I'd designed for the film, and I basically had to recut it. The second time I received notes from a professional Editor, it was another miserable experience.

Once, however, I worked with an awesome and great Editor to help me with a film—Stephen Eckelberry, husband of the late great actress Karen Black. Working with Stephen was a total joy. He taught me some very valuable aspects of Editing, and those lessons have made a dramatic impact on how I edit.

What was the difference in working with Stephen and the previous experiences with the other people? I think it was about how the information was conveyed. In the first two cases, the people I was working with looked down at me and asserted themselves as superior in knowledge. That perspective probably brought an air of tension I picked up on subconsciously, which resulted in my dissatisfaction while working with them. Whereas, with Stephen, he never took on an air of self-importance and instead, even when he was teaching me something new, always went about it as if he was sharing information with a friend. That kind of interaction is lovely and always leaves a nice feeling in the air.

I hope to always carry on an experience of *sharing* with the people I work with. And I encourage others to as well.

I think Editors are useful when they are helpful and want to explore different possibilities with the same thing; and Editors are totally useless when they are stuck in a "my way is the only way" mentality.

When it's time for you to hire an Editor or be an Editor for someone else, remember to create an environment so the experience can be shared in a helpful way.

TALE OF THE EMERALD DIGGER

"What gorgeous gem did you bring me?" Asks the Jeweler.

"It's exquisite," says the digger, "It's the most beautiful stone in the world. You'll never stop thinking about it. You've never seen anything like it."

"Oh, let me see it! I can't wait!"

"Here it is," he says as he unwraps the emerald from a cloth.

"Oh. It's.... It's.... GREEN."

"Well, yes, it's an emerald."

"But nobody has an emerald! Nobody wants an emerald. People love diamonds. They're used to seeing diamonds. They've never seen this before."

"Yes, that's what I said – You've never seen anything like it."

"Well... I can't take it. Nobody will buy this from me."

"Why not?"

"Well it's cut different. It's square. It's green. It's obviously not finished."

"How would it be perfect for you?"

"Well, it'd be perfect if it's round, or marquee shaped, and cut this way, and, well, clear..."

"Oh, you mean – like a diamond?"

"Yes."

The man with the most exquisite emerald has a choice: Sell the emerald to the diamond buyer for next to nothing – or go to the emerald specialty house.

The digger goes across town to the Jeweler who specializes in emeralds.

"What gorgeous gem did you bring me?" Asks the Jeweler.

"It's exquisite," says the digger, "It's the most beautiful stone in the world. You'll never stop thinking about it. You've never seen anything like it."

"Oh, let me see it! I can't wait!"

"Here it is," he says, unwrapping the emerald from a cloth.

"Oh. It's.... It's.... TOO BIG."

"Well, yes, it's the largest emerald on earth. It would make a great necklace."

"But nobody has an emerald this big! Nobody wants an emerald necklace. People love really small and short emeralds. They love emerald earrings. They've never seen this before."

"Yes that's what I said – You've never seen anything like it."

"Well... I can't take it. Nobody will buy this from me."

"Why not?"

"Well it's too big, and too heavy. It's obviously not finished."

"How would it be perfect for you?"

"Well, it'd be perfect if it was small, tiny even, and cut this way, and, well, not so large..."

"Oh, you mean – like earrings?"

"Yes."

The digger takes a good look at his emerald. It probably once belonged to the Pharaohs of Egypt. It is the largest most amazing emerald the world has ever seen – or will ever see. But he's grown tired of walking all over town. He's getting hungry and worn-out. He needs the money to pay for dinner. So he goes home to think it over.

Late that night, the distraught digger goes deep into the middle of town to have a secret meeting with an old jewelry cutter. The digger has one last look at the emerald, admiring its magnificence. And he hands it over. The emerald is cut in half, and half again, ending up in dozens of smaller, tiny pieces – cut exactly like the jeweler mentioned.

The next day, the digger returns to the emerald specialty Jeweler.

"What gorgeous gem did you bring me?" Asks the Jeweler.

"It's exquisite," says the digger, "It's exactly what you want. You've seen this every day. There's nothing shocking here. It's usual, typical. Traditional."

"Oh, let me see it! I can't wait!"

"Here it is," he says as he unwraps the cloth and dozens and dozens of tiny emeralds spill out into a lovely green pile.

"Oh. They're... They're so small... No, this isn't at all what I had in mind."

"Well, but you said people want earrings. You said people want short and small emeralds."

"Yes, but we're going out of business. The diamond jeweler down the street has been taking all our clients. Everyone wants a diamond. We're getting rid of our inventory and stocking up on diamonds. Do you have any diamonds to sell me?"

"No. I'm an emerald digger. I hunt for emeralds."

"Well... I can't take it. Nobody will buy this from me."

"I see."

"Come back to see me when you've got a diamond. Or better yet – where is that huge emerald you brought in the other day?"

"Well, I cut it up, to make it perfect for you, so you'd buy it."

"You idiot! You idiot! You didn't cut up that big emerald to make these smaller stones! Did you? We just got a call from the finest museum in the world. They want to pay big bucks for an emerald like that one. Because emeralds are going extinct! It was one of the last remaining on earth! What with all this diamond craze happening, it would've been the finest emerald anybody ever saw! Oh, that's too bad. What a pity. We really could have made a splash with that one."

WHEN CAN WE SEE IT?

The production of a motion picture is complex. The release of a motion picture may be even moreso! We've received numerous emails asking questions like: "Will the movie be in theatres?" "When can we buy the DVD?" "Will it show in my town (or country)?" and the most often-asked, "When will it be on Netflix?" And these emails have come from Europe, Australia, Africa, South America, North America, Asia. Everywhere!

The motion picture industry has as many layers and middlemen as any other. Perhaps more. Regardless, these people and organizations are a part of the distribution of a film. Each of them represents a tiny segment of the distribution of a film. So unless a film is allied with one of the really large distributors (and we know who they are!) there are a great many hoops to jump through, and people to work with, to begin the process of getting a film on the big screen, iTunes, Amazon, Hulu or Netflix.

Most of us are familiar with the blockbusters that open on 3,000+ screens on the same weekend. By the end of several months, the films have shown in every country of the world and the Netflix debut is eagerly awaited. In between those two platforms the films appear on airplanes, make a buck on an archaic DVD release, then cable channels and satellite feeds. These are all unique channels of distribution. Unfortunately, the world of independent cinema doesn't follow such an all-encompassing path, unless, of course, you are Angelina Jolie with your directorial debut.

In traditional archaic sequential order, the distribution of a film might follow these steps: 1) theatrical release, 2) cable and satellite, 3) travel networks such as airplanes and cruise ships, 4) commercial television, then 5) Online streaming such as Netflix. This can happen in each and every country in the world, either simultaneously (like that seen by the blockbusters) or one at a time over the course of a number of years. Naturally, the commercial goals of any filmmaker might likely include widespread release.

In addition to being a great art form, filmmaking is also a business. Most of us have never stopped to consider exactly how a movie is released and all the possible ways that it can happen. I know I didn't. Furthermore, I never stopped to think about how it might not even be the same exact film in each different country. Oh, it will be mostly the same, but poster art changes, sometimes the title of the film is changed and there may well be editing within the film, depending upon customs and standards in a given country.

My first film, *Pep Squad*, was a satire on American school violence. The script was written in 1995 – long before any of the school violence had occurred – and actually predicted what was to come. We were in negotiations with a major distributor to release the film the very day that the Columbine shootings happened. The company called us immediately and said, "Sorry, we can't touch this now with a ten-foot pole." All of a sudden, poking fun at the American culture and confronting the causes of school violence –

the causes that no one wants to talk about such as parents, bullies, and the society at large – wasn't commercially viable, especially in a comedy! *Pep Squad* had a message that the "society at large" didn't want to hear.

What followed was interesting. All of the domestic distributors were afraid to put *Pep Squad* out there. Some made their own watered-down versions. But the international marketplace was hungry for the film, especially one that detailed and gave insight to what was happening in the US. *Pep Squad* was released theatrically in a number of countries and still continues to show in places such as France and Germany. It has appeared twice on French satellite television, and seven years after its production in 1997 it was released in Germany. In 2011 when the rights came back to me, I gifted them to Lloyd Kaufman (Troma) as a Christmas gift. And today, 23 years after its initial debut, *Pep Squad* is still being released globally.

In North America it sat on the shelf. Finally, when enough time seemed to have lapsed after Columbine, *Pep Squad* was released direct to video after several small theatrical engagements in Los Angeles and other cities. Alas, it was marketed as a horror film, even though it was obviously a satire. Why? Because the distributor believed that its commercial viability was still threatened if taken as subversive commentary on the social problem of school violence. While I disagree with this approach, I do understand how they came to that conclusion. As we all know, art is often defined and categorized because of the culture that surrounds it. Around the world, *Pep Squad* is seen as a hilarious commentary on the absurdity of America, but in America it can only be tolerated if it is labeled an otherworldly horror film.

Explaining the business of distribution is complicated and

difficult. To summarize, a film can be released theatrically in New York, but not Los Angeles; in Ohio but not Florida. Films can be seen on airplanes; on cable; on Netflix; in classrooms; at colleges; in small fine arts theatres; on the internet; throughout many continents – but not necessarily every country; and even if seen in every way possible, films may not be shown in all of those venues all at once. The average lifespan of a film is almost endless. Films from 20 and 30 years ago are routinely showing on regular television.

Distribution is probably the single most misunderstood aspect of the movie business.

MARKETING: YOU VS. THE BIG BOYS

For a single Hollywood studio movie, millions of dollars will be spent on advertising and marketing campaigns to make sure that everyone *everywhere* knows about the movie. It might seem outrageous, but really, they *must* spend that much to have a chance to recoup the massive and absurd costs of making said movie.

For anyone spending less than a million dollars on their movie, there is hardly any money to make a dent in the world of studio-sized marketing campaigns. You might be able to afford some kinds of advertising, but still you will be faced with a huge goliath standing in your way. Without tens of millions, you will be relegated to marketing your movie in a certain niche.

Those of us who make movies for a fraction of that have even less. So what can we do to compete with the big boys? How can we get our movies talked about? How can we get people to see our movies? You do not need stars or money. You just need promotion. After all, people won't watch your movie if they don't know it's an option.

But how can you do promotion with little or no money? By

thinking outside the box!

My dad (Clark) runs a construction equipment attachments manufacturing business called Dymax. To illustrate an example of how you can compete with the big boys, let's explore what Dymax achieved at MINExpo in 2004.

In the world of construction equipment attachments, Caterpillar and Komatsu reign like movie studios Sony and Warner Brothers. For MINExpo, Caterpillar and Komatsu each spent millions of dollars on their exhibits, which were enormous (maybe 10,000 square feet or more). Dymax had only $10,000 to spend. And their booth was maybe about 200 square feet.

Clark asked himself, "What can we do to stand out from the crowd? What can we do differently?" MINExpo was taking place in Las Vegas... What about something involving showmanship and an over-the-top spectacle? But, MINExpo is for miners. Rough and tumble customers.

After thinking outside the box, Clark created a Dymax Sideshow, featuring The Enigma who swallowed swords, breathed fire and stuck nails into his skull; Selene Luna performed strip tease; and Pleasant Gehman (Princess Farhana) did bellydance and burlesque.

The Dymax Sideshow performed every two hours. The Enigma, Selene and Pleasant walked around the exhibition floor and many people took notice. Everyone who saw them felt the urge to come see them perform. Find out what all *that's* about.

Dymax had a steady stream of people stopping by to have their pictures taken with the performers. Most of all, the audiences enjoyed the performances.

When it was all over, Clark discovered that the MINExpo management had awarded Dymax two prizes for Best Marketing. Out of a total of seven prizes handed out to the entire Expo. And it was done for a small percentage of what the big boys spent.

Use this example as a lesson on how to stand out, create your own "buzz" and how to succeed by being creative *within* your limits. Sometimes people are limited by money, by location, by weather, by you-name-it. I see limitations as a blessing. Once you identify your limitation, you don't have to think about it anymore. Instead of thinking about what you don't have, try asking yourself how you can achieve the desired results with what you DO have!

When it comes to design, there are no rules. There is, however, such a thing as bad taste. Bad taste on purpose can be a great way to communicate your product—especially if it's a campy satire. But if you've made a gothic horror or character drama, you don't want to have crappy looking artwork.

There is a tendency in the movie business to create Key Art that looks like the latest hit. There is also a tendency in the movie business to create Key Art that is totally misleading, just so the company can make a buck when the film is released.

My film *Firecracker* could be cataloged as a Gothic horror. Although it is far from a horror film. Nevertheless, the distribution company had the idea of marketing it as a horror film, with blood dripping off the letters and so forth. That was a horrible idea. I fought them and got them to release the film with the Key Art I originally designed, which communicated honestly the atmosphere and tone of the film.

My film *Casserole Club* could be cataloged as a drama, or character study. It has some campy moments (it takes place in 1969, so the costumes and art direction lend itself to looking campy even if the subject matter isn't funny at all), and might have some sexual situations, but there really isn't anything *sexy* about it. The distributors for that film wanted to market the film as a *sexy* and *titillating* soft-core exposé. I thought that would be a horrible mistake because the people expecting to see a sexy and soft-core movie would likely be totally disappointed. Why did they want to market it that way? Because sex sells. That's why.

My thinking is: if you want me to make and then sell you "Babes & Bikini Bingo: Summer Camp" or "Haunted Killer Carnival, Part 3" I'm happy to do so, but don't do something dishonest by marketing a movie that isn't the movie.

When you design your movie poster, it is important to remember that although different fonts can sometimes look cool, they do not look cool when you place them all together at the same time. I always cringe when I see a design that features more than two or three different fonts. It's a dead giveaway that the designer just discovered Photoshop when you recognize the urge to use every font they could find.

I try and keep fonts simple and usually only use two. One font is used for the main title, and another for actors' names, blurbs, and other copy. I try and make sure that the font I use for the main title is not used anywhere else in the design. Using it more than once diminishes the impact of the main title. I usually always find a complementary font to use for everything else. Remember: less is more.

With regards to the image or visual art, think about a memorable moment in the film and use it. Before someone sees your movie, they don't know what that image means, but after they see your movie, next time they see the artwork, it'll remind them of your movie. I try and avoid showing something if it's giving too much away. For instance, if your movie is a murder mystery you probably wouldn't want to reveal the killer on the cover holding a knife, because it would ruin the viewing experience. Maybe if you wanted to throw off the viewer, you would show each character holding a weapon—then the viewer won't know whodunit.

Saul Bass was a great designer of movie posters. You might want to look him up. His designs were far from the traditional Key Art you see today. In this world of Black-Market Punk Rock Film Distribution, Key Art that is actual *Artwork* might be the perfect idea.

The Industry's unhealthy obsession with The Billing Block I may never fully understand.

The Billing Block refers to the collection of names and credits that are positioned at the bottom of movie posters and advertisements. Usually they are composed on fonts with tall and very narrow, vertical lines. So small and tall and narrow that most anyone cannot read them. In fact, it is safe to say that probably no one ever reads them except the people who are included in The Billing Block.

I agree, without The Billing Block, your movie poster looks unfinished or under-designed. Just like all those laurel wreaths from awards or film festivals. No one stops to read the text inside each laurel wreath. People might see the words *official* and *selection*, but hardly anyone can see the tiny words underneath that read: Billy Joe's Steakhouse BBQ Film Festival. It doesn't matter. Having the ability to put laurel wreaths on your movie poster, or in advertisements, makes it look to the consumer that your movie is the movie they should see. The Billing Block has this same worthless effect.

To make a Billing Block, one should start with the name of a production company like: "Paramount Presents" and then have a little space and follow with "a Steve Balderson film" or whomever. Then, you'll list your top actors who have, in their contracts, agreed to be in your movie so long as their names appear *before* the main title, on individual title cards (these are moments in the movie when no one else's name appears on the screen at the same time). Following them, you'll type in the title of the movie. And then a short selection of supporting stars (or other actors who have agreed to be in your film so long as they get their own title cards). Following them will be a list of crew people: editor, writers, art direction, the cinematographer, and maybe someone else, or a producer, and ending with the director. And repeating the same words that were the start of your Billing Block.

Who reads Billing Blocks? Who on Earth can even see that small? Nobody. Well, nobody except people who have their names in The Billing Block. God forbid someone who expects their name to be in The Billing Block can't find their name. O, the unjust insanity.

Placement is an integral part of The Billing Block. Some actors specify in their contracts they must have the *third* placement. Or, the *first*. Or the *second*. I've never heard of anyone asking for the fourth onward. Sometimes people will negotiate that they want their name listed first and will gladly take second position but only if on the same title card as the first person. Even if their name will appear second on The Billing Block.

Size of the font is also a big deal. If the star is at a 12-point font size, typically the supporting cast will be at a 10 or a 9 or 8 font size. Usually this is because the main star gets their own title card, whereas the supporting actors are sharing their card with other names. Making it so their font size is smaller to keep room for multiple names.   There are some actors who specify in their contracts their name must be written in the same font size as the main star.

Twice I've made my name (as director) a half font size larger than everyone else in the credits just to make fun of it all. I'm not one to flatter myself with endless on-screen credits.   Even if I did the costumes, make-up, set design, cinematography, writing, and editing, and whatever else, I think it's tacky to make certain everyone else knows it.   Usually I just stick with "produced and directed by" and leave it at that.

There are people out there who do want EVERY credit they can get. That's fine. Might as well give it to them. It'll keep them quiet and you won't have to listen to them. At the end of the day, nobody cares. I mean, right now, think about it. Which name is listed first on The Billing Block for *The Avengers*? Which name is listed second on the credits for *Star Wars*?

WHAT FESTIVAL PREMIERES MEAN

One of my consulting clients recently asked me to help her clarify the difference between the various types of film festival premieres in order to help her analyze her film festival strategy.

She asked, "What are World Premieres as compared to, say, Regional and/or Local Premieres? More specifically, can I have a local premiere or a U.S. Premiere before the World Premiere, or is there a specific one that is supposed to happen first?"

Filmmakers and the media throw the word "premiere" around so often in the film world, I can understand how it can sometimes be confusing. We're not talking about the red carpet "premieres" that a major studio might have in London, New York, or Los Angeles that have nothing to do with a film festival. Those types of "premieres" are usually held for publicity purposes to kick off a global theatrical release.

At film festivals, when you have a World Premiere, that means it's the first time your movie will screen publicly in the world. Some film festivals only accept films with World Premiere status, such as Sundance. If you have already screened at another festival prior, you could be disqualified from participation. Some film festivals do not require a World Premiere status. It's important to know their rules before you submit your movie. I advise people to submit to the festivals that require a World Premiere first, because you can always submit to the other festivals later.

Likewise, there are festivals that require a country or regional kind of Premiere Status. A US Premiere is the first time the film screens publicly in the US, and a NYC Premiere means it is the first time the film is screened in NYC, and so forth.

My consulting client continued, "A Chicago festival that runs in mid-October is where I want to be the official Premiere of my short film...but...an L.A. festival that I also want to submit to is hosting their event during the first week of October and their notifications of acceptances/rejections are released two months before the Chicago notifications. If I get into both festivals, can I still designate the Chicago one as a 'World' premiere even if I already screened in L.A. a few days prior? Also, does any of this premiere lingo (world, U.S., International, Regional, LA, NY, East Coast, West Coast, Midwest, etc.) used at festivals, to distinguish one premiere from another premiere, really matter?"

I always suggest entering as many festivals as you can. Sometimes one is limited by funding (if you entered all of them you'll spend tens of thousands on submission fees). If you get accepted into two or more festivals that each require a World Premiere, you always have the option to decline being in the less desirable one. In this case, I suggested if she gets into both the LA and Chicago fests, to screen in both. I don't see the trouble in saying your World Premiere is in Chicago—especially if the LA screening date was just within a few days of the Chicago date.

The use of the word "premiere" via film festivals themselves is meant to promote the festival itself. If they can tell their regional newspapers that they have movies that have never before been seen in St. Louis, for example, then the festival might draw more of a crowd. A message like that sends the signal to come see it because they may not get another chance!

When my movie *Casserole Club* got into Raindance, we had to promise it would be a UK Premiere, but they didn't care whether or not the film previously screened in the US, etc. When it came time to see if we could get into the Berlinale, Berlin said we couldn't be considered because we'd already screened at Raindance. They wanted a World Premiere (or at least a European Premiere). Now, had I been accepted to both Raindance and Berlinale, and had their dates been closer, I might not even mention Raindance, and if Berlin found out, I could have told Berlin that the Raindance screening was an unfinished test screening, or "Sneak Peek" and that the "finished" movie would premiere at Berlin for the first time, making it a World Premiere. (I haven't tried that kind of scenario yet, so I'm not sure if it would even work, but it seems plausible to me and Berlin might buy that).

Lastly, I think any "premiere" lingo is really about marketing, and festivals just want to make sure they have ticket-buying customers.

THE SUNDANCE DISEASE

My dislike for Sundance has nothing to do with the original message of Sundance. I genuinely think Robert (Redford) had a great idea. The original concept is beautiful and very valuable, celebrating filmmakers of all sorts. But in recent years it's distorted beyond recognition. Sundance is now a gargantuan disease infecting the world and it's time to confront it. We can no longer be in denial.

The first cases were diagnosed in Los Angeles, leading the CDC to theorize that neither Robert (Redford) nor Park City, Utah, was the source of The Disease. I interviewed a Studio Executive suffering from The Disease. Said individual stated, "You are nothing unless your film is shown at Sundance. If you aren't at Sundance, you must not be a real filmmaker." All other research indicates that most films "accepted" into Sundance have, in one way or another, been financed, produced, or planned by a company in The Industry.

What happens to the real independent film? What happens if one doesn't surrender? The same thing that happens to people in our culture that don't fit the mold! They are exiled! They are called freaks! Which reminds me of the scene in FREAKS: "One of US! One of US!"

Have you been in contact with The Sundance Disease? How would you know? Here are signs to look for. Common symptoms include: Confusion and general disorientation characterized by a preference for freezing temperatures, deep snow and high altitude instead of warm waters, white beaches and the mild climate of Cannes in May; Preoccupation with Sundance participation on the part of the inexperienced public who have no knowledge of important festivals such as Berlin, Toronto or SXSW; Industry Wannabes who insist that missing Sundance dooms a film to second class status.

A secondary infection of The Disease is the marginalization of all the other festivals. It makes all the other organizations less important: "Oh, you got into Cannes – too bad you weren't 'accepted' into Sundance!"

Slamdance started with good intentions and challenged the bureaucracy of Sundance. Now, Slamdance has developed symptoms of The Disease. And, if we aren't careful, it will spread to Slamdunk and all the other Dances. Remember what happened to LapDance!? At this rate of infection, we'll be looking at TromaDance to predict the 2006 Oscar nominees. We'll have forgotten all about the Independent Spirit Awards.

The Disease is as contagious as SARS. And, like SARS, there is currently no known cure. But if all independent filmmakers fight together, we can stop it from killing us.

An earlier version of this story was originally published in Aftertaste Magazine, 2004.

STEVE BALDERSON

WE SEE WHAT WE KNOW

But, do we know what we see? I don't think we do. The other day I received a stunning photograph of my nephew. Maryann Bates, an award-winning photographer and nominee of the Pulitzer Prize in Photographic Journalism, had taken it. When I sent it to my family, my brother responded with "I'll fix the glare so it'll be ready for print."

I laughed, because this is a trait amongst our family. My grandfather was this way; my parents are this way, my siblings, cousins, and myself to some degree. We could watch the greatest performance on earth by any given artist and know deep down how it could've been better.

But then I started to think about it. Backlighting (the process by which a light source is placed behind someone's head, to give a glow around the edges, almost like they have a halo) is a classic trick in romantic photography. The practice of backlighting has been used endless times by the world's greatest cinematographers, portrait photographers, and painted by the Renaissance masters.

Yet, in this instance, the art of backlighting had been

misunderstood and somehow defined as something needing to be corrected. Was it possible that my brother hadn't learned of backlighting? Perhaps he's never seen backlighting used in any photographs or artwork before. This is hard to fathom but it does make sense and brings me to wonder about how I see things.

When I look at something, I know what I see. I take it in, and if it's new to me, sometimes I'm excited, sometimes I'm sickened, but overall, I take it in. I try and learn about it so that I *know* what I'm looking at.

I believe that the majority of the world does the opposite: they see what they know. They see what they *already* know. If they see something that they've never seen before, they might define it as *bad* or a *mistake* or something that needs *correcting*. By correcting the thing, they change what they see into something familiar to them, something they already know about. Once that unknowable thing has been categorized into a thing they feel comfortable with, only then they think they know what it is. Because they can categorize it now.

If someone has never been to an authentic Italian restaurant it is understandable that they believe Olive Garden is authentic Italian food. If someone has never learned about different religions, or traveled abroad, or witnessed cultural diversity, it is totally understandable that they could believe that the entire world is exactly as their own city or town. It isn't their fault their perspective of the world is narrower than others. But it does bring into question what is being taught in schools.

Over the years, as I've worked on different projects, and gained more knowledge and experience, I've learned a great deal about perspective and how movies impact people. I've also learned a lot about how writers, actors, and other creative people feel about things.

One person will say they hate the music while another will say they love it. One person will say the flow of the movie is trance-like, while another will say it's jarring. One person will say that the writing seems forced, while others will say it feels poetic.

There will be sales agents who say these things too. It's pretty common for Hollywood in general to always find something about your movie they hate. You'll see. There will be distribution companies, reps, film festivals, *anybody* and everybody, who will insist their ideas and opinions are fact—and the funny thing is—they will all contradict each other.

That happens every time I get ready to sell a film or promote it at festivals. Every time. And it will likely happen every time for you, too. My advice is to somehow learn how to let it bounce off of you. Keep going. There will be someone, somewhere, who loves it. Prepare yourself for an endless barrage of rejection one after the next. Eventually it will all work out. Keep going until the movie is shared publicly with as many people as possible.

You'll learn that after gathering everyone's opinions, you'll be surprised to see that every element in the entire film will be loved at least once, and also, hated at least once. For every person who likes this, there will be another who hates the same thing and loves something else, which was hated by the other guy. This is just how life works.

Learning all that has helped me identify when a project becomes true to my vision and perfect for me. And that is all I can do. That's all anyone can do.

When I share rough cuts of my films with professional editors in

Los Angeles and NYC, and other filmmakers, and well-known actors who have worked with some of the greatest directors of our time, their opinions don't change my own perspective. I share it with them out of curiosity. Some people need to hear other people's points of views in order to help define their own. I'm not like that. It could be because I'm more visual, instead of verbal or auditory. I'm pretty sure it's all about how the brain works and how each person processes information.

The people who need to hear what other people think so they know what to think are usually the types who hear something negative and try to "fix" it. But, if they did that every time a new opinion came in, there would be nothing left. It would be a big black void with some credits playing. Although, even that could end up gone if someone else didn't like the font.

Of course, I'm always fascinated in hearing other people's perspectives of any movie I make. I'm so proud of a film when I complete it, of course it feels good to feel the pats on the back. It's exactly like being a parent. When your kid makes a good grade or wins a contest, it feels good. And, likewise, when that kid is bullied, it hurts. But bullies are out there, and there's nothing we can do about it as parents.

I'm also aware that, like food, some people may not like the way it tastes. That's okay. Reviews don't teach me how to be truer to my vision. They only teach me how to better appeal to the critic. If I've made a risotto with white truffles, and the person eating it doesn't like rice, there's no way I'll win them over. If my objective is to win that person over, I'll have to make what they like.

If my objective is to have the best Italian restaurant on the block, I need to focus on making the best Italian I can and be true to my vision, instead of worrying about the people who don't like Italian and would rather eat Chinese. And, likewise, if my intention is to create a New Wave Italian, classic Italian purists might not like it.

Be true to your own perspective.

Keep going.

STEVE BALDERSON

A CHAIR IS A CHAIR IS A CHAIR

Have you ever heard someone comment, "My god, that's a *bad* chair!"? I doubt it, as there really is no such thing as a bad chair or a good chair. There are simply different levels of craftsmanship involved in making a chair, and, of course, a variety of finishing techniques and overall aesthetics. Some chairs are spit out on an assembly line by the thousands, while other chairs are made by hand. Some chairs have cushions, some have armrests, and others even have accessories (i.e. little cup holders, rocking abilities, footrests, etc.). In any case, it remains a chair. The purpose of which is to be sat upon.

The people who sit on chairs all share the same activity. They sit. Sure, some people have poor posture, but in general, I can't see how someone could be a good sitter or a bad sitter. Never do people go to a dinner party and loudly complain, "Francis, look at the way you're sitting in that chair! It's *bad*! Just awful!" In fact, it makes me wonder, how, exactly, could Francis be sitting badly? His rear end is fixated on the seat! Both feet are on the floor! Sure, he's got a bad back, which makes him lean a little to the left, but nevertheless, Francis *is* sitting in the chair. The only way, from my point of view, Francis could fail in his sitting, is if he weren't sitting at all! It would seem to me that only when one stands is it appropriate to attack their ability or talent to sit. "Francis, you're *not* sitting!" Perhaps those few people who, in their attempt to sit, miss the chair completely and plummet to the floor, are guilty of poor sitting, but the indignity of missing the chair would seem to be punishment enough, without adding insult to injury by bringing their failure to their attention.

Like the people who fail to sit in chairs, I believe it's only acceptable to attack an actor when he or she has failed to appear in a film. Michelle Pfieffer, for instance, is bad for failing to appear in *The Silence of the Lambs*. Likewise, so are Whoopie Goldberg, Demi Moore, Madonna, Nicole Kidman, Reese Witherspoon and all the other actresses who didn't appear in that film. Shame on them.

Don't get me wrong – some actors look great in any movie, while others do not. Jodie Foster, for instance, looks equally as great sitting in a plush sofa from Eddie Bauer as she does swiveling on an Eames with matching black leather ottoman. Other people, like the late Marlon Brando in his elder years, for instance, aren't necessarily the most elegant of sitters. There are some people, without a doubt, that should avoid sitting on certain chairs. But that is all about looks, not general sitting ability.

Movies, it can be argued, like chairs, are not good or bad – they simply have different levels of craftsmanship. What's the difference in how Thomasville, Broyhill, or Ethan Allen chairs are made? Very little that I can see. Sure, the shapes and textures differ, but they seem to be built in the same fashion. Much like films made by committee, they seem safely appealing to most, and, I agree, manufactured with skill (read: they aren't going to fall apart). Ron

Howard's movies are like these. So are Martin Scorsese's for that matter. There is nothing more or less exceptional about either.

Some chairs, like those sold at Pottery Barn or Crate & Barrel, are constructed with equal skill, but have aesthetics (and prices) that appeal to a different buyer. Clint Eastwood reminds me of Eddie Bauer.

Marketing and selling a motion picture is just like marketing and selling furniture. Pottery Barn needs to sell thousands, if not millions, whereas Eames is happy to sell a few hundred. *Blair Witch*, while poorly made, still sold millions. That movie in particular is just like furniture sold at Wal-Mart. And in retrospect, the people who buy furniture at Wal-Mart are, probably, not going to buy an Eames. And, like an Eames, *Eyes Wide Shut*, while one of the best-crafted motion pictures ever made, didn't appeal to the masses.

Within all of these examples lies genre. The genre of World Market furniture (read: often made with cheap components), tend to fall apart a lot sooner than, say, a Broyhill nightstand, which has the solid construction of a Bergman film.

You can tell what kinds of films people like by taking a look around their living room. What kinds of furniture do they have? Do they prefer to sit upon a chair made of plastic, mesh, wood or steel? Do they sleep on an air bed or a top of the line Sealy? Where do they eat dinner – on the floor, on the sofa, or at a solid oak dining table?

On my street we understand movies are like pieces of furniture. We know what separates a Restoration Hardware from an IKEA. We acknowledge there are similarities and differences. But whether it's manufactured by the thousands or made one at a time, the bottom line is – it's only a movie.

STEVE BALDERSON

DISTRIBUTION MIDDLEMEN

A lot of filmmakers are confused about the realities of distribution, and rightly so. I've been making and selling movies internationally for over a decade, and I'm still learning about all the secrets and tricks The Industry hides from us. Part of the problem is that no one shares this information with each other, both the good and bad, so I'm making it my mission to do so. Openly, honestly, and hopefully clearly.

When your film is ready for release, there are a variety of ways to get it out into the world. There are aggregators and sales reps, producer's reps and distributors, foreign sales agents and a variety of middlemen who can help you.

First, we'll explore just one of those ways.

The Sales Agent.

Sales Agents are people who represent dozens, if not hundreds, of movie titles. They take these films to markets such as Cannes, Berlin, and Toronto. (Film Markets are not to be confused with Film Festivals, which sometimes happen simultaneously and in conjunction to Film Markets). While attending these markets, they rent a booth or a space (such as a hotel room) and invite buyers from different distribution companies from all over the world, to stop by their booth and check out their titles. Sometimes the Sales Agent will aggressively track down certain buyers from different countries with promotional flyers about your film.

Years before they made *Sharknado*, The Asylum was the first Sales Agent I worked with and they were downright brilliant. They are incredibly nice people, they paid their bills, they were actively in touch with us, and sharing with us ways they were selling *Pep Squad*. They managed to sell my movie all over the globe: Australia, New Zealand, France, Germany, Austria, Switzerland, Italy, Scandinavia, South Africa, South Korea, the UK, China, Greece, the Baltic States, Indonesia, the Middle East, Portugal, Thailand, and Turkey. Oh, and even Canada. I can't tell you how sad (okay, devastated) I was the day I learned The Asylum wouldn't be actively selling other people's movies anymore.

Finding a new Sales Agent to replace The Asylum was a bit like being dumped by the love of your life and having to quickly find a new soul mate or risk perishing into the depths of hell forever.

In the process of finding the good guys, I worked with a variety of scumbag Sales Agents selling several of my movies. And I've encountered many that were so full of themselves, and so rude, that I ended up not hiring them.

First, remember that YOU are hiring a Sales Agent. They aren't hiring you. Their egos are sometimes a problem. To keep their egos well fed, they will often treat you badly so you think you *need* them, when in all honesty, to keep in business, they need *you*. If they don't have your film on their roster, they'll have to find someone else's film. They cannot afford to remain in business if they aren't selling as many movies as they can.

The second lesson is to beware of Sales Agents' so-called "marketing expenses." I've been to the Cannes. I know for a fact it doesn't cost several hundred thousand dollars to be there.

Most Sales Agents will pad their "marketing expenses" so they can fly First Class, put themselves up at the Carlton, or Hotel du Cap (well over $1,000 a night) and dine at the "in" places, with tasting menus featuring 20 courses, wine pairings, and more. Yes. That's what they spend their money on. Or, your money, rather. They don't use it to sell your movie. They think they should be treated like royalty and will try and convince you as much.

Sales Agents will sometimes pay you an advance when they acquire your movie, but then as they sell it to different buyers, they keep all the money that comes in until they recoup their "marketing expenses." Unless you've read the fine print and capped their expenses, you may never see another cent beyond the advance.

I prefer not getting an advance in exchange for the Sales Agent taking a commission on all sales, and giving me my shares from the first dollars in. When you're signing an agreement with a Sales Agent, be sure to discuss this aspect openly.

A client once asked me, *"Is there a set fee or a range that filmmakers can expect to pay sales agents? I once considered joining a distribution co-op that consists of a group of filmmakers collectively promoting a catalog of films to buyers...their fee at the time was two thousand dollars."*

I replied: WARNING. There is no fee for a sales agent. I'm not sure what kind of co-op you were thinking about joining, but that sounds fishy to me. I've never paid a sales agent. I don't know anyone who has paid any kind of fee to a sales agent. Sales agents pay *you*. I'm automatically skeptical of anyone asking for money to help sell your film. However, if the co-op you were talking to was asking $2,000 to cover expenses related to releasing your film straight to consumers, and skipping the sales agent route, there might be something to that. But I'm not sure what.

Say your sales agent (let's call him Bill) wants to take on your movie and he says, "I loved Acts Two & Three, they were so great I cried, but Act One is boring." Remember to ask yourself, "What does that communicate to me about Bill?"

Did he watch the film late at night? Early on a Saturday morning. Was he drunk or hung over? Was he tired? Was he awake? Was he hungry? Did he feel Act One was boring because he didn't yet realize the tone of the movie? Was it because he hadn't seen the press kit? Or perhaps it was because he simply didn't care about character development and wanted it to start with a bang? Any of those situations are plausible.

Bill probably doesn't understand that one of the reasons he loved Act Two & Three so much was because of Act One. If one starts watching a movie in Act Two, there is no kind of care for the characters and no emotional connection to them.

Perhaps Bill is incapable of getting to know someone, which would suggest that he probably jumps right into sex without even going on a date to test out the chemistry first.

You do not need Bill's advice on how to make a movie (though he will disagree). You need his advice on how to find the right buyer and get into the right festivals. Remember that.

Always remember to stay on topic when people like Bill offer feedback. By saying "that's something to consider" it puts the topic to rest and allows the rest of the conversation to continue.

Another kind of middleman is the Producer's Rep. A Producer's Rep is a person who acts as a negotiator for your film and his or her sole purpose is to get your film sold to a Sales Agent, Aggregator, or Distributor. They will hold private screenings (you'll pay for it, naturally), they'll send out post cards or other materials (you'll pay for those too), and they'll do a bunch of other stuff (some useless) you'll need to reimburse them for as well. Sometimes they'll do things that don't require reimbursement, such as talk to people on the telephone. Eventually, when they make a sale, they will take a percentage of that sale as commission.

There are many people out there who call themselves Producer's Reps. Some of them are failed Industry executives. Some are failed filmmakers. A few are attorneys and only a couple actually know what they're doing. All of them claim to know everyone in the business, and most of them will require a retainer before actively taking on your film. Those are the kinds of Producer's Reps to avoid. Instead, find one who works solely on commission. Those kinds of Producer's Reps are very rare, but they will try harder to actually sell your movie. Producer's Reps that have already been paid a retainer of, say, $5,000, don't really have an ambition to make a good sale since they've already made some money.

The first Producer's Rep we hired was a disaster. We'd stupidly paid him a retainer (not knowing we could otherwise have found someone who would take commission), and he just didn't have the ambition to get the job done. The longer he didn't sell the film, and the longer we paid him, the more reason he had to *not* sell it. We believed everything he told us, which was naïve, I know, but he had been a former VP of Acquisitions at a major studio. So why *wouldn't* we believe him?

The thing about Producer's Reps is that they aren't willing to do anything that rocks their boat. If they were too aggressive, their relationship with Studio Head X, or whomever, would be damaged, so they aren't going to be an aggressive salesman. They'll pussyfoot around delicately so they can always look good in the eyes of the buyers they have relationships with.

Like most people in The Industry, Producer's Reps will act as though you work for them. They will somehow totally deny the fact they are, in reality, working for *you*. Once I asked our Producer's Rep to share with me his contact list (mailing addresses, etc) of buyers at each company. This information is publicly available. It isn't secret. You can make a telephone call to every distributor and ask the front desk, "Who is the name of the Acquisitions personnel?" and they will tell you. It's easy. But it takes time to call them all. Maybe not days and days, but I wanted to save time, so I just asked our Producer's Rep for his list.

He was flabbergasted. He flew through the roof. How dare I ask him such a thing! He said, "It's my livelihood, I can't share that with you." I informed him that anyone can make that list, that it was just going to save me some time. But he was the wise and experienced one, and I was some filmmaker from Kansas, what did I know? Of course, he didn't take me seriously and share his list.

So, I did the research on my own. It took a couple days, but in the end, I'd gathered the data and had my list. When I told him I had my own list, he actually asked me to share it with him so he could make sure his was up to date. Was he kidding?

I think that was the last time I spoke with him. A few weeks later we sold the film. Perhaps he helped. Or, perhaps it was my list and the marketing strategies I did on my own (without his help) that ended up selling our film. Who knows.

I haven't used a Producer's Rep since that first experience, and I continue to sell movies without using one, so I'm not sure there's any reason to hire one. But if you do, be aware. And beware.

Lastly, we have the Distributors and the Aggregators. A Distributor is a person (or company) that takes your movie and gets it out to retailers like RedBox, Netflix, Amazon, iTunes, cable and satellite, on-demand, and other VOD platforms. Aggregators are the people (or companies) who Distributors use to assist them.

Filmmakers have caught on, and now more and more are approaching Aggregators directly instead of using a Distributor. And it makes sense. Aggregators will keep their commissions and marketing expenses before paying dues to the Distributor, who in turn will keep their commissions and marketing expenses, before paying their dues to you (or before paying their dues to your Sales Agent, who in turn will deduct their commissions and marketing expenses, before paying you). So why not cut out all the middlemen and hire an Aggregator from the get go?

It isn't that easy. In fact, it becomes even more complicated.

If it were easy for filmmakers to get their films to an Aggregator directly, half The Industry would be out of a job. Distributors would become obsolete. This will be the eventual outcome, but in the meantime, Distributors everywhere are trying to hold on to their jobs. So, naturally, Distributors are making it appealing (financially or otherwise) for Aggregators to work with them, instead of you and me. Today, Aggregators aren't set up for one-on-one relationships with filmmakers. As technology advances and makes it possible for more films to be made, the strain will continue to weigh on Aggregators who don't morph their company structures to suit.

Any musician can post their music to iTunes and sell directly to their fan base. As of today, iTunes is not open for any filmmaker to upload their movies. Right now, filmmakers must use a Netflix approved Aggregator in order to get their movies on Netflix. My hunch is that the moment Netflix opens its doors to filmmakers, directly, as iTunes did with musicians directly, that is the end of the Distributor and potentially the end of the Aggregator.

If Aggregators are to survive, they'll need to morph into a kind of Distributor, which essentially, brings an entirely new dilemma. Then there are the Aggregators out there who will take on any project, no matter what it is, for a fee.

I make movies for my audiences. I do not make them to appeal to Industry executives, Distributors or Aggregators. And I'm not going to waste money paying an Aggregator to do something today I'll be able to do without them tomorrow.

If an Aggregator or Distributor tells you there isn't a market for one of your films because they didn't like it—ignore them. Get your movie out there any way you can. There are VOD platforms you can get on besides Netflix. And when the day comes these VOD platforms are open to filmmakers directly, you won't need to worry about an Aggregator or Distributor ever again. You'll be able to provide your product directly to your audience. Just like the music industry.

Our fan bases and audiences around the world do not care who releases our movies, or what companies have been involved in getting our movies to their desktop, TV or iPhone. Our audiences just care that they can watch whatever they wish... in whatever form they want.

MOVIES LIKE REAL ESTATE

When a person goes to sell or buy a house, there is a very clear asking price to begin negotiations. I think movies should be treated and sold the same way.

This, of course, doesn't apply to mega studio super budget movies that are all done in-house and have nothing to do with the rest of the world. I'm talking about independently made films seeking distribution.

Say you've made a movie for $75,000. I think it's best to just say it. If you try to make it sound like your movie is worth $750,000, you might look foolish. Likewise, if a typical three-bedroom house in Kansas costs $350,000 and you're asking $1.2 million, you are likely not going to sell your house.

Of course, there are dumb shits in the world who will pay for something that costs more than its worth. But even though it seems those types of people have the run of the place; they really are quite rare. I suggest finding out what your movie is worth on a realistic level and just tell people that's what you want for it.

If you say you want $75,000 for worldwide rights, expect an offer for anywhere $50,000 or even lower. If you're selling worldwide rights, that would be the end of the deal. No royalties, nothing else. There is a lot of greed out there, naturally, so people would rather "lease" their movie, or "rent it" like they would a residential property. But, I say, if you can just sell the damn thing and move on—do it.

Of course, location has a lot to do with selling a house. For instance, a $300,000 house in Kansas would be worth about $3.2 million if it were located in Los Angeles, or $15 million based on the same square footage in New York City.

Think about your movie in terms of genre and star power. If you have Julia Roberts in your movie, you'll likely be able to ask millions for it even if it only cost $100,000 cash to make. Do you have a Victorian mansion, or a two-story duplex, or a mid-century modern ranch-style? Is the home you're selling in a desirable neighborhood, or is it on the wrong side of the tracks? Is it a horror comedy, coming of age drama, or musical?

You can try and disguise your movie all you want, but at the end of the day, it might help you to understand your movie from a realistic perspective. Bring in someone to evaluate the worth of your film and strategize the best way to get it out there.

If you've made a movie for $75,000 it might serve you better to release it yourself. For that amount you only have to sell 4,000 VOD purchases. That isn't a huge ordeal. But, on the flip side, if you've made a movie for $300,000, you'll have to sell 15,000 VOD purchases. While that's not out of the question, it's a lot easier to sell less. So, keep your costs as low as possible. Or remember that if you are selling a home, it's best to get as much as you can and then move to a town where you can get a lot more for a lot less.

EXPOSURE OR MONEY?

Because of my interest in eating well, I've known many restaurant owners. Once, I asked a maverick restaurateur why her bottles of wine were priced less than other fine dining establishments. She confided in me that her main objective was to move more product. Her goal was to sell twice as many bottles of wine than her competition. So, she priced them affordably. Usually the markup is ridiculous. A $12 store-bought bottle of wine usually costs $12 per glass at a restaurant. Though she'd price the entire bottle at $22.

I used to struggle with this idea until I started realizing what my preferences were when it came to releasing movies. Often times, people will ask me which of my films has been the most successful. It's a really hard question to answer. First, I have to ask them what they define as success. Everyone has an entirely different definition. Some people define success as the amount of money a movie makes, while others might define success based on the critical acclaim, awards, exposure, or in how many countries your movie is released.

My film *Firecracker* was released in almost every country on the planet, won numerous awards, pre-eminent film critic Roger Ebert gave it a special Jury Prize on his list of that year's best films, yet the investors never made a decent return on their investment and in the USA it was basically shelved by the stupid distributor and is currently only available for streaming at Vimeo On Demand at this link: www.Vimeo.com/ondemand/firecracker

Wellspring was a really hip distribution company who wanted to distribute *Firecracker*. The company is now long gone, but at the time they were the coolest boutique place to be. They were distributing Todd Solondz' movies at the time. Wellspring offered a decent advance, but only wanted to print 10,000 DVDs. While another distributor, First Look Studios, was offering a little less money but planned to release 100,000+ DVDs on the initial run. We decided to go with First Look.

For me, at that time in my career, it was more important to have the volume and exposure, even if I was setting myself up for less financial reward.

When it comes time to release a film, I always ask myself which is better: to release the film globally, in as many countries as possible, for potentially less return? Or is it better to have a smaller release in just a few countries and make a lot of money? Each movie has a different set of criteria and a different set of questions and answers.

Of course, we all want as many people as possible to have the chance to see our work. And we also hope for great financial return so we can continue to make additional movies. This is why it's important for me to keep costs as low as possible. That way, I have a greater chance of financial reward.

Some of you might not know that exhibitors take 50% of any ticket sales at the movie theatre. So, if a studio movie cost $50 million to produce and market, they will need to have box office returns that exceed $100 million before they'll ever see a cent of profit. If you've sold your movie to a distributor, the distribution company will take even more, so the likelihood is you'll need a box office figure closer to $150 million.

If your independent movie has a chance to make about $250,000 worldwide over the course of a lifetime, it might behoove you to keep the budget for that particular project about a third of that or lower. The Movie Business is a business, albeit an idiotic and incredibly limiting one. But it can be incredibly rewarding and successful on many levels. Just depends on what you define as success. And how you'd like to share your work with the world.

STEVE BALDERSON

WAITING TO WORK

If you are serious about wanting to get your film actually made, you should avoid Hollywood altogether. Trust me. No one but The Majors make movies in Hollywood. The players you would think would be the most involved are precisely the individuals least interested in the activity. What? How can you say that? Well, because it's true! People go to Hollywood to be in a continuous state of development. Why? BECAUSE THEY ARE LAZY. They do not want to work. They do not want to be productive. They want to stay in bed or lounge about the fucking pool sipping martinis.

No one in Hollywood will return your calls because there's just no time! They will tell you they're SO swamped. People in the movie business are SO busy. Try so busy scheduling their August holiday! Think you can call back in September? Guess again! From September to November people in the movie business can't manage a conversation because all capable speaking skills are being sucked up by Toronto and the other fall film festivals. No one works in December, regardless of religion, and when they return after the New Year, all available time is spent obsessing over Sundance. And, of course, February is out of the question because everyone is obsessed with what happened or didn't happen at Sundance.

April through May is lost to Cannes. This leaves only March and a slim chance to reach anyone during hiatus (June and July). Unless you've got *Spiderman* 7 in the works, or the latest special effects show, the only real chance you've got is to make your film on your own. Think you want to involve The Industry? Heed this warning!

There's nothing wrong with enjoying time off from time to time but must we remain *off* so much of the time? And what are people doing in their off time? Playing videogames, chatting with online strangers, playing golf, attempting yoga, gorging on wine and cheese? Whatever happened to productivity? Come to think of it, maybe Hollywood isn't the only place contaminated with laziness.

There are 365 days in a calendar year. 104 of them are wasted by people not working on the weekends. That only leaves 261 days to get any work done.

Think it stops there? Guess again! We can't forget the holidays! (FYI: The movie industry observes every holiday known to man, and not just the major ones. I used to think they did this to avoid offending any major cultural or religious group. But, it seems to me that most everyone in the U.S. does it as well—even people who are deliberately offensive on a daily basis and clearly cannot be attempting to avoid offending someone!)

We have Martin Luther King, Jr. Day, Lincoln's Birthday, Washington's Birthday, Good Friday, Memorial Day, Flag Day, Independence Day, Labor Day (by all means a special day to deliberately not work!), Columbus Day, Election Day, Veteran's Day, Thanksgiving, Christmas... and those are just the Bank Holidays!

We can't forget Chinese New Year, Groundhog Day, Valentine's

Day, Ash Wednesday, Purim, St. Patrick's Day, April Fools, Passover, Easter, Tax Day, Kwanzaa, Nurses Day, Mother's Day, Armed Forces Day, Father's Day, Rosh Hashanah, Yom Kippur, Halloween, All Saint's Day, Eid al-Fitr, Hanukkah, Ramadan, and, of course, Cinco de Mayo!

I found the following on the website for the Pennsylvania Department of Banking: *"When a fixed holiday falls on Sunday, it shall be observed on the following Monday; when it falls on a Saturday, it may be observed on the following Monday. Independence Day, July 4, will fall on a Sunday and, therefore, must be observed on Monday, July 5. Christmas Day, December 25, will fall on a Saturday and, therefore, may be observed on Monday, December 27."*

Are they kidding? No! We wouldn't want to overlap a weekend with a holiday for a chance at yet another day off!

By the time New Year's Eve rolls around, people take yet another two days off! Yes, two whole days. (No one should have to work with a hangover!) I've never understood why people celebrate the coming of a new year. Are they excited yet *another* year has passed? Are they thrilled at the notion that in the coming year they only have 24 days to work? Or, are they thrilled at the idea that 341 days will be spent not doing ANY?

On my street, there isn't a reason to take a vacation. We don't need a break from our lives. We need no escape. We happen to enjoy what we're doing. That's a rare thing these days—actually having enjoyment at your place of work.

I used to get really frustrated. It seemed that every time I turned around people were finding any excuse possible to avoid doing any work. Now, I see it as a gift. While millions are sitting around by the pool, playing golf, taking a holiday, the rest of us can get the upper hand. My advice is to encourage other people to take even more time off from work. This way, you will be able to accomplish more while they're gone. And if you are efficient, you might even reach your desired results before everyone else gets back.

If, on the notion you dislike your life and don't really want to do any work, I suggest moving to Los Angeles and getting a job in the movie industry. If the move seems daunting, taking any job seems to do the trick regardless of the location. Don't worry. You're sure to find a place where you don't have to do anything!

LES DELIVERABLES

After your film is complete and you've licensed it to a sales agent or distributor, you will need to deliver them a shit load of things—some of which are important and some of which are totally unnecessary. They call these things "Deliverables."

Years ago, filmmakers had to gather and deliver twice the amount of crap we need to deliver today, a lot of which costs thousands of dollars to produce. Sometimes this made projects go over-budget, into debt, and people had to borrow money to pay for all the items. There wasn't a way out of it, because if we filmmakers wanted our films distributed, we needed to cough up all the deliverables they asked for. Well, that isn't totally true. Sometimes a distributor asks you for something that truly they do not need until they make a sale.

Let's say your sound mixer didn't do an M&E (separate tracks for music and effects, which makes it possible to dub dialogue in various languages overseas). If you're a newbie (like we all were at one point), you might panic (like I did) and spend several thousand dollars on creating an M&E simply because they ask for it on the list of Deliverables. My advice is to save the money. Tell your sales agent or distributor that you're happy to pay for an M&E when the time comes, so long as the sale will cover the cost of making it.

If a distributor in Europe wants to buy the rights to your film for release in Germany, say, and they want an M&E so they can dub the film in German, make sure the sale of those rights exceed the cost of making an M&E. Or, tell them they'll have to release it with subtitles (which might make them reject the deal and not buy your movie). It's a risk, but in my experience, I've never had a deal not go through under these circumstances.

Likewise, when a distributor asks me for "Textless" movie or trailer files, I almost always disagree. That means they can change the title. And if they do want to change your title, chances are it'll be changed to something pretty lame and embarrassing.

Other Deliverables are: photocopies or scans of actor's agreements, contracts with crew, copies of music and score licenses, time code charts of music cues, dialogue transcripts (of spoken dialogue, not what was written in your script), proof of copyright, stills, behind the scenes footage, and lots of other stuff. I get why they want all this information, but gathering it takes time. My advice is to gather it along the way so that when it comes time to deliver your Deliverables, you'll have everything ready.

Never be afraid of saying you don't want to deliver something. If they ask for unmixed sound files, for instance, I never give it to them. Because then they'll have the actual sound files to certain effects and sound design that was created specifically for your project. Paul N. J. Ottosson, the Oscar-winning sound designer I mentioned earlier, worked on one film of mine where the distributor wanted his unmixed files. There was no way I was going to share his secrets. It just felt totally wrong to me. So, in my agreement with the distributor, I simply took a black marker and crossed out those items on the Deliverables list. You can do this too. Worst-case scenario is they come back and tell you it's a "must" or else they won't buy your movie. My hunch is they won't care. I never had a problem with that.

STEVE BALDERSON

CARRY ON

When asked about the secret of his success and long career, actor Michael Caine answered: "I have a policy. I never listen to anyone explain why they *can't* do something. I don't want to be convinced by them."

How often do you encounter people with such negativity that it influences you? Have you ever been driving with someone who said, "We'll never find a parking spot"? Next time that happens, turn to them and ask, "Never? Ever again?" Sometimes people decide things that limit them without even thinking. And in that limiting decision, they have created a negative energy that surrounds them—and you.

On a movie set, when someone shouts "it'll never work" or "we don't have enough time" just tell them to leave the room. There's no reason to be in that kind of environment. I like to think, "there's always a way to make anything work" and "there's plenty of time." One just needs to be creative. It is very difficult to be creative when you're concurrently making a limiting decision about something.

I taught one of my consulting clients about how he could make a short film. Months later, I learned that he had indeed made his short, and that the film was accepted to screen at the Cannes Film Festival. Isn't that wonderful? I'm fairly certain he didn't make any limiting decisions along the way.

If you're a worry wart and are often experiencing or creating difficult situations in your life, it might be hard to grasp this idea. But it is the case that any kind of negativity reflects in everything you do. What you project comes back to you. Therefore, it is always beneficial to operate without any limiting decisions and to always surround yourself with positive thoughts.

Try removing the following words from your daily dialogue: *can't, won't, never, don't.* I practice this exercise daily. My favorite was the first time I experienced an entire week without saying the word *don't.* Instead of telling someone what you don't want, you'll find it is always easier to tell someone what you *do* want. At first this might seem challenging, but you'll get the hang of it.

The subconscious mind cannot process negatives. Here's an example: *Don't picture a blue tree.*

What is the first thing you pictured? A blue tree! And even if you immediately changed the color of the tree, you pictured a blue tree even when I told you not to. Don't imagine a baby crying. Don't imagine a birthday cake. Don't imagine an orange rose. More of the same. Whoever decided the famous billboard should use the words "Don't drink and drive" is an idiot. It is far more effective to use the positive intention with the words "Find a sober driver."

Anyway, when it comes to communication—whether on a film set, during writing of the screenplay, or in ordinary day-to-day life—be conscious about what you're saying. Are you telling people what you want? Or are you only expressing what you don't want?

Everybody knows show business has less to do with talent and more to do with the connections you make and the ones you can use to your advantage. However, when I suggest that it's all about who you know, I mean—when it comes to life in general. Who you know, and who you surround yourself with, will affect the quality of your life and your work.

If you surround yourself with people who are chaotic, angry, shallow and unpleasant, you will live a life that is chaotic, angry, shallow and unpleasant. If you surround yourself with people who are centered, mature, and full of inspiration, you will live a life that is centered, mature, and full of inspiration.

After leaving film school, I surrounded myself with people who were very dramatic, very catty, and sometimes incredibly bitchy and shallow. I also had friends who were centered, calm, and interested in visiting about the bigger picture. I didn't know it at the time, but what was happening was this: when I was around those creative artists, I too felt inspired to create. And when I went out to dinner with the shallow and superficial person, I experienced the world as she saw it. It was a miserable friendship and I didn't even know it!

The quote from Michael Caine I mentioned earlier: "I have a policy. I never listen to anyone explain why they *can't* do something. I don't want to be *convinced* by them."

It is true that other people's beliefs and behaviors impact each of us. How many people are in your life that drive you crazy? Do you have people in your life that inspire you? Who are they? How often do you seek to be around people who enrich your life, instead of take away from it?

Sure, some troubled people might be "going through a phase." That's fine. But ask yourself: how does their "phase" influence you?

Is it better to remove yourself from their sphere, so you can live your life on YOUR terms, or is it better to live your life in theirs? Every troubled person is a good person deep down, and with the help of therapy and deep introspection on their part, they might be able to evolve. If you are unhappy in any situation involving anyone else, ask yourself: how many days and years of your life will you waste being swallowed up by their troubles?

TELL THEM YOUR NAME

If there's one thing I've learned in my 23 years in this industry that has helped me more than others, it's this: when you see someone you know at a film festival or premiere, reach out to shake their hand and before saying anything, tell them your name. Even if you know they know you. Even if you just saw them last week. Especially do it if you haven't seen them in a while. Why?

People who work in the entertainment world meet more people in one year than most the general public meet in their entire lives. And unless you're a political wizard (Bill Clinton is rumored to remember every single name/face he's ever met), there is no way to remember everybody. Trust me.

I was naïve once, many moons ago, when vacationing at Canyon Ranch in Tucson, I met the director Joel Schumacher, who was also staying there. We had dinner, hours of great conversation (him giving me advice mainly), and then kept in touch after we left. The next time I visited Canyon Ranch, he was there again. What a coincidence! We had dinner again, more advice, more great conversation, and it was awesome. Then, the next time I went to

Canyon Ranch, would you believe it, Joel was there again! This was beyond bizarre and such a weird coincidence that when I walked past him the first time, I said something funny, like, "God, Joel, are you moving in?" Of course, he didn't think it was funny and confronted me for saying it. When I reminded him of our history together, he apologized but then explained to me that although I remembered our last meeting as if it were yesterday, he had no idea who I was at first. It was only after I reminded him that he remembered. Then, he explained to me the advice I'm writing about today.

Now, over a decade later, I know exactly what he meant. In any given year, I travel to film festivals, screen films in various cities, give workshops, meet old friends, new friends, I've worked with hundreds of actors and crew people in my films, I've met hundreds of others, and I can tell you that it is impossible to remember everyone at any given moment.

Have you ever had that feeling, walking through the grocery store, and running into someone you knew years before and you can't quite place them? Maybe you went to school with them, elementary or college, or, maybe they worked tables at your favorite restaurant, or maybe they were friends with one of your siblings and you saw them around from time to time. But, because it's been long enough, you have absolutely no idea how to place them, and how you know them? Do you know that feeling? Well, in the entertainment world this is ten-fold.

When I'm at an event for one of my films and a thousand people are there, I am overjoyed when someone tells me their name upon first seeing them. I really love it when they follow up their name with how we know each other.

I was speaking for a university class recently and stuck my hand out to meet the professor and said, "It's nice to meet you," at the exact same time he said, "Good to see you again." Then I asked how we met, and he replied, "I was in one of your films." I was shocked and embarrassingly asked, "Oh? Which one?" I mean, you'd think I would know if I was talking to an actor I'd previously directed. He explained that he was an Extra in a film which was shot 10 years prior. I was relieved that he was just an Extra and my embarrassment vanished. It's hard to keep track of Extras.

What the hell do you do when someone comes up to you and doesn't introduce himself or herself, and you have no idea who the hell they are?

I'd suggest asking them who they are, or how you know each other, but, I did this once and it had a dreadful outcome. Right after I asked, this person replied, "I'm surprised you can't remember. We once dated for a few weeks." I replied, "Oh. I... Sorry, I... about that, see..." and went on to explain how people who work in show business meet more people in one year than most people meet in their entire lives. This sounds like such a silly excuse to use in real life, but it's true.

To avoid any kind of sticky situation, my advice is to simply say, "It's good to see you." And smile. This sentence works if you know the person *and* if you're just meeting them for the first time. If you're at an event showcasing your work, like a premiere, or whatever, it's good to follow that up with, "Thank you for coming" or "Thank you for being here." Those words will always work in your favor.

Now, if the other person persists and continues to have a detailed conversation, and you still have absolutely no idea what they're talking about, you could always change the subject into a topic universally fresh – such as the purpose for the event you're both attending. Or, if you truly want to avoid the person, pretend to get a phone call and excuse yourself. No phone handy? A trip to the loo might take care of that.

Likewise, if you're in a situation with a person whom you totally remember but can't stomach talking to—like a stalker or something—the best reaction is to still say, "Good to see you, thank you for coming," before walking away from them. If they follow you, you can always alert security.

Another great plan of action is to have a pal present who can save the day. A secret sign or gesture, a code word perhaps, could alert your friend to spring into action and drag you away for an important matter that needs addressing immediately.

The bad part about the reverse situation is being taken advantage of. See, I know many people who have very famous friends. I've met some of these very famous people, but there are others I haven't. If I wanted to meet these other very famous people, I could just walk up to them, introducing myself as "We met at so-and-so's movie, party, or fill-in-the-blank." And I guarantee you that very famous person won't actually know whether we really met or not.

I don't think this is a very bright idea, but it could actually work if you know all the right people and are familiar enough to carry on a short conversation long enough to be photographed standing next to them for some stupid Wire Image shot.

Working in show business might have a lot of perks, but sometimes by being in public it opens up a huge can of beets that no one really wants to eat.

PRIORITIZE YOUR TIME

I'm aware that our modern world isn't easy to navigate. I know people have jobs, bills to pay, the need to put food on the table, shuttle kids to and from school or band practice or play practice or that sports game. I get it. But, if you're really good at time management, you can do all this *and* write scripts, make movies, and so forth.

I know it's possible to write a screenplay in less than a week and get paid $15,000 for it. I know because that happened to me. I also know that I'm incredibly meticulous in time management when it comes to something like that. If my goal is to write a script in a week or so, and I'm getting paid 15 grand for it, I know that there is no time to waste at the gym, or on the phone chatting with friends, or texting and tweeting the latest news.

I don't think twice about just shutting the phone off or telling friends and family that I'm going back in the "writing cave" or the "editing cave" or whatever. Most people appreciate it and respect that and understand the situation.

Other people don't understand it, and that's when it can become problematic. Everybody has a needy friend who has a personality that if you don't return his or her call or text immediately, they take it personally and think you're mad at them. Then, by the time you've re-emerged from the cave, your friend hates you and you don't understand why.

Well, I'm here to say, screw 'em. Needy people are trouble. Ask yourself which is more important? Do you want to finish your script, your edit, your work or your art—or do you want to make sure you're holding on to social obligations that have nothing to do with supporting your goals? True friends, and people who support you and your goals, will always be there for you, regardless. I say "screw 'em" to the rest because they'll eventually just start sucking out your life force like leeches.

Now, I understand it's easy for me to go into a creative cave of any sort because I don't have pets, I don't have children, and I'm not keen on frivolous social obligations with people I barely know. I've made the decision that right now is the part of my life where I need to focus on myself.

Scheduling is also an important part of managing one's time. I can totally juggle the responsibilities of earning a living, putting food on the table, and also creating art. You might not be able to do them all at the same time. Sometimes it's possible to block out two hours a day for writing, or nine hours a day for earning a paycheck, or one hour a week to write a blog article. But, unless I write it down in my planner, and keep to the schedule, it becomes impossible to manage everything.

Some of you might be gifted when it comes to time management and scheduling yourself. And some of you might really struggle with it. My only advice is to make it a habit. I think it only takes something like two weeks to make something a habit. Start small, by getting a daily planner or learning how to operate the calendar on your smart phone. Set alerts for yourself.

Most importantly, ask yourself if there are any activities or choices in your current lifestyle that impede your ability to work on your art or reach your goals. Are some of those things necessary? Can you do without them? Or, if you must have them (say you aren't ready to give Fido up for adoption), can you think of ways to keep those items and *also* achieve your goals?

There's no excuse to avoid achieving your goals. There is simply time management and figuring out HOW you can achieve them no matter what.

STEVE BALDERSON

DENNIS HOPPER'S HOUSE

Pulling up to his compound on a side-street in Venice Beach, California, not far from the beach, I was struck by the surreal corrugated metal façade. If I hadn't known he lived there, it would make sense that someone offbeat did. And the white picket fence out front, planted firmly with tongue in cheek, was the perfect touch.

My dad, Clark, was with me. We were ushered in the front door and navigated a seemingly endless row of classic cars, luxury cars and more cars. At the end of the parking area we climbed a flight of stairs that was open to the second floor, with an enormous ceiling probably 50 feet high. As we climbed it became brighter and brighter, and I took notice of the original Warhols, Basquiats, and other incredible pieces of modern art. Later I would learn that his collection was vast. Dennis explained that he shot two bullet holes through Andy Warhol's portrait of Mao Zedong. And, instead of Warhol freaking out about it, he called Hopper "a collaborator."

At the top of the staircase I was surprised at how plain his house was. Just one big space with dining area on one side and sitting area on the next, kitchen beyond, and a doorway to the bedrooms.

Hopper's then wife, Victoria, was in the kitchen and greeted us as Hopper came in wearing sweats and a hoodie.

I'd brought him a gift. A coffee table book of photographs called Backyard Visionaries. Dennis grew up in Kansas, down the street from my grandmother's home in Dodge City. He loved the book.

The first thing he told us was that he thought *Firecracker* was one of the best scripts he'd ever read. I presented him with my storyboards of every shot of the entire film. He carefully read it, commenting how amazing this film would be.

He said he'd love to be part of the film and then we settled back to speak about life and other interests. Dennis had been in negotiations with Lehman Brothers (the former global financial services firm) to produce 10 feature films for $10 million each. Lehman would bankroll the venture for $100 million and Hopper would be in charge of the slate. Hopper asked if we could use *Firecracker* as the first of these projects. I was over the moon. "Of course we could," I said. And we shook hands.

(Eventually the Lehman deal fell through. I was told that Lehman changed their offer to Hopper and said they only wanted to put up $50 million, telling Hopper he had to come up with the other $50 million. He told them to forget it.)

At some point during the discussion Victoria turned on the television and we watched in horror as reports came in that the Concorde had crashed on takeoff in France. My sister and I had flown the Concorde back from the Cannes Film Festival. We talked about how incredibly small it was inside and how anyone over six feet tall couldn't stand up straight walking down the aisle.

Dennis Hopper was a fascinating man and a super nice guy. He was complimentary of my work and gave me some damn good advice. It's a shame we didn't have the chance to work together before he became ill. When I learned of his passing, I took a moment to remember the Backyard Visionary he was when he started out making art and movies, and I smiled.

STEVE BALDERSON

ADIOS, KAREN

I first met the actress Karen Black in 2001 when I stopped by her house to try and persuade her to star in *Firecracker*. She knew I was coming, so she let me in. I was instantly transfixed while watching her body movements and facial expressions. There was something about her entire being that reminded me of a wild cat... like a panther or a jaguar. She seemed to float on the air, feet never touching the ground.

Karen eventually agreed to star and we went about making the film. She was an incredible trooper on set. One of my favorite scenes is when her character leans out the window to talk to the young boy. When it was time to reverse the camera and get the kid's shot, it was nearly 5am and we'd been filming since long before sunset. Several people on the crew were worried about getting Karen back to her room so she could sleep but she stood firm and refused to go. She wanted to stay and be there to act with the kid who was being filmed. For *his* shot. She was a total pro.

In the years after, Karen and I remained good friends and I'd look her up every time I was in Los Angeles. We always daydreamed of another project and when we would be able to work together again.

In 2008, Karen was being honored at the Macon Film Festival and they were to show *Firecracker*, so I was flown in to present it with her. It was such a lovely town, we decided to make a movie there. Karen said, "I've always wanted to be in a women's prison movie and no one's ever asked me to be in one. Isn't that peculiar?" So we decided to make *Stuck!* together.

At first, I'd thought of casting John Waters' muse Mink Stole as the part of the Next-Door Neighbor Lady, and Karen as the bible-beating shooter on death row for gunning down an entire fleet of tax collectors. Karen really wanted the part I had in mind for Mink, and eventually I convinced Mink to take the part I'd originally had in mind for Karen. It ended up being a great switch, and both women were perfect in their roles.

I was my own camera department and DP for the film. One of my favorite moments during the filming came when we were shooting a scene near the end of the film where Karen's character is riddled with guilt. In that room, on the set, we turned to each other after a take and looked around. It was just the three of us. Karen, me, and my sound guy. I made the comment about how amazing this was, this exact experience. How intimate and real and honest. She smiled, looked me deeply into the eye and said, "Now THIS is filmmaking."

APPENDIX

DAY/DATE

"Call" means camera ready (M/U, hair, costume done)			**CREW today:**
Actors today:			**(director)**
NAME (CALL TIME)	NAME (CALL TIME)		NAME (asst)
NAME (CALL TIME)	NAME (CALL TIME)		NAME
NAME (CALL TIME)			NAME
NAME (CALL TIME)			NAME

Props: (and other special needs)

TIME			
15:00 – 3	SCENE	Scene name, descriptions, directions.	Character names in scene
15:15	NO's		
15:30			
15:45			
16:00 – 4			
16:15			
16:30			
16:45			
17:00 – 5			
17:15			
17:30			
17:45			
18:00 – 6			
18:15			
18:30			
18:45			
19:00 – 7			
19:15			
19:30			
19:45			
20:00 – 8			
20:15			
20:30			
20:45			
21:00 – 9			
21:15			
21:30			
21:45			
22:00 – 10			
22:15			
22:30			
22:45			
23:00 – 11			
23:15			
23:30			

Any important notice to remind you of a special need the next day

THURS, SEPTEMBER 22

"Call" means camera ready (M/U, hair, costume done)			**CREW today:** SB (director)
Actors today: ADEELA MICK JACK		BIG GUY (8 PM)	MPage (asst) A1 (sound / cam2) NO TOM James Merchant

Props: "Bonnie" video, pendent, Big Guy's rifle

14:00 – 2			
14:15			
14:30			
14:45			
15:00 – 3		CALL = **MEET IN ROOM**	
15:15		District or Circle Line to Victoria	
15:30		Victoria Line to Oxford Circus	
15:45			
16:00 – 4	60/61	Street post kidnapping	AMJ
16:15		(LOCATION: Portland or Wardour Mews)	
16:30			
16:45			
17:00 – 5			
17:15			
17:30	62	Tiny Alleyway – undies/pendent	AMJ
17:45		(LOCATION: Portland or Wardour Mews)	
18:00 – 6			
18:15			
18:30		Dinner at: Breakfast Club: 33 D'Arblay St, W1F 8	
18:45			
19:00 – 7		(There's an EAT on Soho Sq)	
19:15		(Inamo: 134-136 Wardour St, W1F 8ZP)	
19:30		Central line to Lancaster Gate	
19:45			
20:00 – 8	64	Street on the move to find computer	AMJ
20:15		(LOCATION 203-211 Sussex Gardens)	
20:30	65	Townhome	AMJ, Big Guy
20:45		(LOCATION: 235 Sussex Gardens)	
21:00 – 9			
21:15			
21:30	66	Street post Big Guy	AMJ
21:45		(LOCATION: Talbot Square)	
22:00 – 10		**WRAP**	
22:15		Walk to Paddington, Circle Line back to SJP	
22:30			
22:45			
23:00 – 11			
23:15			
23:30			

Starina leaves LAX on Virgin Atlantic Flight 8 at 5:35 PM her time

ACKNOWLEDGEMENTS

Filmmaking involves intense collaboration with many people, and in the past two decades I have had the good fortune to work with some of the most creative, talented and generous people on this planet. To every one of them, I owe a huge thanks. I'm not going to name names, because I've seen what happens when someone is missed. You who have been on this journey with me know who you are. I love you. I value your friendship, your counsel, your wisdom and all that you have given to me. What I am today is an amalgamation of your presence in my life. To each of you... Thank you from the bottom of my heart.

ABOUT THE AUTHOR

Preeminent film critic Roger Ebert gave Steve's film *Firecracker*, starring Karen Black and Mike Patton, a Special Jury Award on his annual Best Films of the Year list. His first film *Pep Squad* premiered at the Cannes Film Festival at Le Marché du Film then became a 90s cult classic. In 2011, the U.S. Library of Congress selected his film *The Casserole Club*, starring Kevin Richardson of the Backstreet Boys, for its permanent collection. In 2015, his film *El Ganzo* won Best Feature, Best Actor and Best Cinematography at the Salento International Film Festival in Italy.

Film Threat magazine says, "Balderson makes movies that are so gorgeous that it's not unreasonable to say that, cinematographically at least; he's the equal of an Argento or Kubrick in their prime. Some people have perfect vocal pitch, Steve has perfect visual composition."

Interested not just in film but also architecture, design and elements of time and space, Balderson's milieu is all-inclusive and his work bears an unmistakable, individual stamp. Though he chuckles when he says his idea of a good time is 'going out to sketch a story board,' he's not kidding. Driven and prolific, in 2018 Balderson directed his debut music video for Jane Wiedlin of The Go-Go's.

More information about Steve Balderson can be found on the websites www.SteveBalderson.com and www.DIKENGA.com or by searching his name on the internet.

www.ingramcontent.com/pod-product-compliance
Lightning Source LLC
Chambersburg PA
CBHW021358090426
42742CB00009B/909